THE ILLUSTRATED HISTORY OF THE
RATROD

STEVE THAEMERT, JR. WITH RICK LOXTON
PHOTOGRAPHY BY CHAD TRUSS

i-5
PRESS

The Illustrated History of the Rat Rod

Project Team
Editor: Amy Deputato
Copy Editor: Joann Woy
Design: Mary Ann Kahn
Index: Elizabeth Walker

i-5 PUBLISHING, LLC™
Chairman: David Fry
Chief Financial Officer: David Katzoff
Chief Digital Officer: Jennifer Black-Glover
Chief Marketing Officer: Beth Freeman Reynolds
Marketing Director: Will Holburn
General Manager, i-5 Press: Christopher Reggio
Art Director, i-5 Press: Mary Ann Kahn
Senior Editor, i-5 Press: Amy Deputato
Production Director: Laurie Panaggio
Production Manager: Jessica Jaensch

Library of Congress Cataloging-in-Publication Data

Thaemert, Steve, Jr.
 The illustrated history of the rat rod : the people, the cars, and the
culture / Steve Thaemert, Jr. w ith Rick Loxton.
      pages cm
 Includes index.
 ISBN 978-1-62008-196-9 (hardback)
1. Hot rods--Customizing--History. I. Loxton, Rick. II. Title. III.
Title: Illustrated history of the ratrod.
 TL236.3.T44 2015
 629.228'6--dc23

                        2015021089

This book has been published with the intent to provide accurate and authoritative information in regard to the subject matter within. While every precaution has been taken in the preparation of this book, the author and publisher expressly disclaim any responsibility for any errors, omissions, or adverse effects arising from the use or application of the information contained herein. The techniques and suggestions are used at the reader's discretion and are not to be considered a substitute for veterinary care. If you suspect a medical problem, consult your veterinarian.

i-5 Publishing, LLC™
www.facebook.com/i5press
www.i5publishing.com

Printed and bound in China
18 17 16 15   2 4 6 8 10 9 7 5 3 1

CONTENTS

Introduction

There's no question that rat rod culture is surrounded by a lot of "gray area." For every fact, there seems to be a million opinions—opinions often formed through misperception or even bad information. And while this gray area sometimes creates confusion about what a rat rod is or where the term came from, it's also part of the rat rod scene's charm. Rat rods and the rat rod culture leave a lot of things open to interpretation. Some elements of the culture simply can't be defined, while others are so subjective that they are entirely different for each person.

In this book, we'll try to sort through the myths and get to the facts of what a rat rod is, what rat rod culture truly represents, and where this movement came from. I've written many articles in response to the question "what is a rat rod?" and I'll probably write many more. It's the question I've been asked most often throughout my tenure as editor of *Rat Rod Magazine*, and it's the popular "pot-stirrer" in online forums. Want to get people talking? Ask them what a rat rod is. People naturally love to share their opinions, and their opinions are flavored by their own needs, ideas, and experiences.

Again, this is the charm—and possibly the biggest downer—of rat rod culture.

I'm not here to define anything. No single person or idea can do that. Only the community of builders and enthusiasts who collectively make up the rat rod scene can define exactly what a rat rod is. And even though people argue about and lobby for their own personal views on what a rat rod is, the culture tells us exactly what it is already: a rat rod is a blue-collar hot rod. Period.

Now, regarding that fact, there is a lot of room for interpretation, but the roots of rat rodding will always be deep in hot rod history. A rat rod is a form of hot rod, and the two cultures run parallel even today—maybe even more so today than in the past. The term "rat rod" may not have surfaced until the 1970s or '80s (no one really knows for sure), but the rat rod mentality has been around since the creation of the automobile. And, as with the automobile hobby, the terminology used in the rat rod hobby has changed over the years. What we considered a rat rod back in 1960 is much different from what we considered a rat rod in 1995, and both are much different from what we'd consider a rat rod today.

The automotive world is always evolving—cycling and recycling trends and fads, flowing alongside culture, living and dying and living again with each generation. The beauty of rat rod culture—and hot rod culture in general—is that it's so rooted in American history that it endures. Its multigenerational appeal carries it from fathers to sons to grandsons, changing along the way but never deviating too far from its foundations.

Preservation comes in many forms. In the automotive world, you have museum-quality restorations—which are an important part of history—all the way down to the daily driver. Yes, you can certainly drive a piece of history; in many cases, that is the best form of preservation because you are maintaining it and people are seeing the vehicle in motion in a very real way. The thing about expensive restorations is this: once you restore a vehicle, its original story is covered up forever. Take a faded '33 Chevy sedan with all of the dents and scratches on its patina-laden body. Its story is there, in those imperfections. Maybe it has a bullet hole. Why is it there? Did it come from a couple of kids shooting targets in a field, or was this car used for a bank robbery, or … what? Patch it and paint it, and that mystery is gone. Same with old lettering or historic markings. Cover them up, and you can no longer see the story. In rat rodding, these imperfections are usually preserved. The story is left visible for each observer to interpret.

So, yes, the rat rod community is essentially preserving vehicles—albeit in an unorthodox manner. But doesn't it make sense to leave some history alive in all of its distressed beauty? Time is an incredible artist. So is Mother Nature. They work in tandem in fascinating ways, not just on cars and trucks but on people and really everything around us. Rat rodding tends to capture that artwork and display it.

The exciting thing about today's rat rod and hot rod scenes? You're seeing cars from the 1930s and '40s and sometimes earlier that have sat for decades in scrap yards or in fields and have been resurrected and given new life. I think it's fascinating that a seventy-five-year-old car can be patched together and driven around the country, with all of its history—its soul, if you will—preserved and passed on to a new generation. What a cool way to honor automotive history—by enjoying the very essence of the automobile: the drive itself.

Like *Rat Rod Magazine* has done since 2010, this book will take you on a visual journey into rat rod culture—from its roots to its modern manifestation.

PART I
ROOTS AND HISTORY

i
Early Influences

The automobile. It's hard to imagine a time when we couldn't jump in a car or truck and head off down the road. The first legitimate steam-powered automobile was built in 1768, followed by the first car powered by an internal combustion engine in 1807.

It wasn't until 1886 that the first gasoline-powered car was produced in Germany. From there, the first production vehicles hit the market; by the early 1900s, there was an automobile boom in Europe and the United States.

Henry Ford launched the Ford Motor Company in 1903 after leaving his first company—the Detroit Automobile Company, which later became Cadillac. By 1910, gasoline-powered cars were being produced by the thousands. Rat rodding has roots here, in the "vintage era" between 1918 (the end of World War I) and 1929, when the stock market crashed. The Ford Model T was the dominant car during this time, and many of these original bodies are still used today throughout the hot rod world. While rat rods didn't exist back then, the Great Depression of the 1930s pushed Americans into creative uses of the automobile. This "forced ingenuity" led to the birth of the "doodlebug."

When tracing rat rod culture in search of its roots, it would be an injustice to overlook the doodlebug. Like "rat rod," the term "doodlebug" also has its gray areas and different interpretations. The definition that's relevant to rat rod culture describes automobiles turned into farm implements (sometimes called "doodlebug tractors") during the material shortages and economic hardships of the Great Depression through World War II. Farmers often took their family vehicles and modified them to be used for plowing fields, hauling loads, or serving any number of purposes for which they were not originally built.

The American doodlebug is a symbol of automotive ingenuity inspired by necessity, a remnant of which lives on in today's rat rod community. Like those who created doodlebugs in the past, rat rodders of the modern era often repurpose parts and components that are rare, broken, irreplaceable, or simply used for purposes other than those for which they were intended.

Gas Power

Karl Benz, of Mercedes-Benz lineage, produced the first gasoline-powered automobile in 1886: the Benz Patent Motorwagen.

The need for such functionality was very obvious during the world wars as well as during the Great Depression, but during the early automotive boom, there was also another growing element: the need for speed.

Mother Nature has programmed every living being with the drive to be better, faster, and stronger than his neighbor. Therefore, it makes sense that the invention of the automobile was followed closely by automobile racing. The earliest documented "races" were more like endurance trials to prove that these newfangled machines were capable of making it from point A to point B with a minimal amount of trouble. This was no small feat, considering that there were few roads as we know them today. Automobile owners gave no thought to modifying these early vehicles because the point was to prove their roadworthiness as-is.

Fast-forward a few decades after the automobile had become a part of everyday life for the majority of American households, and you'll find that automobile racing had become immensely popular. The races had morphed from cross-country endurance events to competitions held on oval tracks. What had once been a hobby for the super-wealthy was now within reach of a wide audience because there was now a rich supply of old cars in junkyards to use as raw material.

The aftermarket as we know it today did not exist, so there was no available "bolt-on" horsepower to make home-built racecars go faster. In fact, people were doing just the

An original 1930 Ford Model A.

A vintage photo from the early days of car racing.

opposite. The less weight you had to move, the faster you could go. By removing things like lights, fenders, doors, and glass, you could free up the available horsepower to move the vehicle forward with more urgency. These racecars of the common man were known as "jalopies," and jalopy races were a mainstay of the American racing scene from the 1930s until well into the '60s.

Take a look at an early hot rod, and you can easily see the jalopy influence. The modern-day rat rod definitely takes cues from the old jalopy racers. The parallels are simple—low cost, do-it-yourself, vintage iron. Many people refer to rat rods as jalopies today, which is almost a slang use of the term, but somewhere in that sea of gray, the dots do connect. Doodlebug, jalopy, hot rod, rat rod … all part of the same automotive culture that was born well over a century ago.

So, where does hot rod culture begin? Rat rodding, after all, is a part of hot rod culture.

What we commonly refer to as the hot rod culture started to take off in the 1920s and '30s as automobiles became more common (as opposed to a luxury of the rich and privileged). The price of new cars was declining, and used cars could be found rather cheaply. Junkyards and used-car lots began to spring up, offering inexpensive entry into the fraternity of car ownership. Hot rod culture and jalopy racing are close kin, and, along with the necessity of the doodlebug, these automotive ideals all ran parallel.

Some saw the car as more than just a means to get somewhere. They saw the car as a way to explore the world, to have fun, and to express one's self. Inspired by the popularity of automobile racing, owners began to tinker with their cars, finding ways to make them perform better, go faster, and look different from everybody else's cars.

By the end of the 1930s, manufacturers had abandoned the "form follows function" approach to designing automobiles and began to put a lot more thought into how cars looked. They had flowing lines and graceful curves that easily lent themselves to further augmentation and customization. It is here where hot rodding began to diverge into two paths. There were those whose main goal was speed, and there were those who saw the automobile as more of a showpiece. For the latter group, everything had to be finished and shiny, and performance (outside of general "streetability") became secondary.

A classic hot rod at on display at a vintage car show.

Above and beyond everything, the automobile represented freedom. If you had a car, the world was yours to explore. The rebel element of hot rodding was always there from the beginning. Deserted highways and dry lake beds were common gathering spots for those wanting to prove their mechanical skills and manhood by driving their modified cars faster than the rules of the road would normally allow. Adrenaline junkies—both drivers and spectators—craved the intoxicating rush of high speeds coupled with the ever-present specter of danger. Those choosing to cruise rather than race formed car clubs with aggressive-sounding names like "The Diablos" or "The Phantoms," suggesting that their group was one to be reckoned with.

The advent of World War II put a hold on the further development of the culture as the call of duty sent a great percentage of America's young men into the service. On top of that, everything related to automobiles was being rationed as part of the war effort. Gasoline and tires were very difficult to obtain, and there certainly wasn't much of anything available for something as frivolous as hot rodding. America's car manufactures even ceased the production of civilian automobiles soon after the attack on Pearl Harbor, meaning that there are few 1941 models, even fewer 1942s, and no production automobiles for the years 1943, 1944, and 1945, with regular production resuming for the model year 1946.

A pair of Ford coupes from 1939 and 1940 at the 2015 Lonestar Round Up show for cars from model year 1963 and earlier.

Once soldiers began to return from duty, the hot rod culture picked up where it had left off and then exploded. Guys coming back from the war had three things that fueled this

rebirth: disposable income, a plethora of new mechanical skills, and the pent-up desire to get back to doing what they loved. And then it happened: rock and roll music.

The country's youth had never had a common voice, but they found one with this exciting, albeit taboo, new music. The kids were driving mysterious-looking loud cars and listening to what was called "the devil's music," and the teenagers of America were indeed in full rebellion.

As auto customizers stretched their imaginations further and further, a funny thing happened. Detroit began to take notice. The cars of the late 1940s were more or less recycled designs of the late '30s and early '40s. Once manufacturers began to focus on automobile production after the end of World War II, this started to change. Of course, we were also entering the jet age and soon would be entering the space race with Russia. These two factors alone would have a great influence on the cars that would roll out of Detroit during the second half of the 1950s. But there is no denying that the creations coming out of the customizing shops and garages around the country also had an influence on what was showing up in new-car showrooms. Cars were lower and leaner—chopped and channeled from the factory. Paint schemes and interior treatments were wilder than anything that anyone had ever seen on a new car.

A highly modified custom 1951 Mercury coupe.

PUSHING THE LIMITS

Rat rodding at its basic roots is a break from the norm. It shoves its finger in the face of the hot rodding establishment and says, "I'm tired of the status quo." It's all part of a constantly evolving process. The original hot rods and customs were a way for people to differentiate their cars from everybody else's. But, eventually, even those building custom cars needed to further distance themselves from the rest of the crowd. Leading the charge was a man who would become the pied piper of those everywhere who dared to be different: Ed "Big Daddy" Roth.

Roth was born in 1932 in the center of what would become the flashpoint of all things "kool" in the automotive world: Southern California. Roth immersed himself in the SoCal hot rod scene, amassing a collection of cars. His artistic nature led him to his first foray into car customization by learning how to pinstripe. This helped him make ends meet while trying to support a wife and five children by working at a department store during the day. He soon gained a reputation as a gifted pinstriper, and he eventually left the retail world behind to forge an automotive career.

The first car of Roth's that gained significant notoriety was Little Jewel, a mildly customized 1930 Ford Model A Tudor. But it was the invention of fiberglass that cemented Big Daddy's place in hot rodding history. This revolutionary material allowed anybody with enough mechanical know-how and determination to design and build the car of his dreams without having to learn how to perform the metalwork that was previously needed to customize a vehicle. Any design you could imagine was now within reach, and Ed's second creation, The Outlaw, was unlike any other custom that anybody had ever seen. It caused such a buzz that he was able to open his own garage and start cranking out other mind-bending creations, including Road Agent, Mysterion, and the famous Beatnik Bandit. None of these cars (except Outlaw, for which an argument could be made that it was loosely based on a 1920s-era Ford) were based on production vehicles. They were all from the mind of Ed himself.

Building these cars wasn't cheap, and much of it was financed with the airbrushed T-shirts that Ed sold at car

Kustom Kulture

The use of the term "kustom kulture" was born of Southern California roots sometime in the '60s and was generally used to describe the hot rod lifestyle as a whole. Although kustom kulture has evolved over the decades, it has always had an artistic and rebellious undertone. The term (and improper spelling) is still used today to describe the '50s, '60s, and '70s hot-rod lifestyle.

shows. Images of his grotesque monsters, often shown piloting equally wacky custom cars, were selling just as fast as he could create them. His most popular monster was Rat Fink, which was intended to be a direct jab at the wholesome, clean-cut Mickey Mouse. Rat Fink was everything that Mickey Mouse wasn't: bloated, dirty, smelly, and just plain ugly. The word "fink" in the character's name was a slightly less vulgar derivation of another term used to describe someone of, let's say, less than altruistic values. The outrage that these shirts caused only served to exponentially broaden their—and Ed's—popularity. Model-car kits based on his creations sold by the millions at the zenith of their popularity.

Ed's interests eventually turned to building custom motorcycles and three-wheeled "trikes," but his initial visions helped usher in a new era of free-form car customization. Other luminaries of the day, such as Dean Jeffries, Gene Winfield, George Barris, and Darryl Starbird, also began to shift their focus from more traditional, organic designs to more fanciful, abstract creations with features such as asymmetrical pieces and bubble tops. Roth, along with Kenny Howard (better known by his nom de plume, Von Dutch) could also make a case for creating the primordial ooze that eventually evolved into what is now known as the "lowbrow" art movement.

Lowbrow Art

Lowbrow art became popular in the 1970s and referred to the pop surrealism movement that was heavily influenced by hot rod culture, punk music, and "comix" (underground, self-published comics).

2
What Is a Rat Rod?

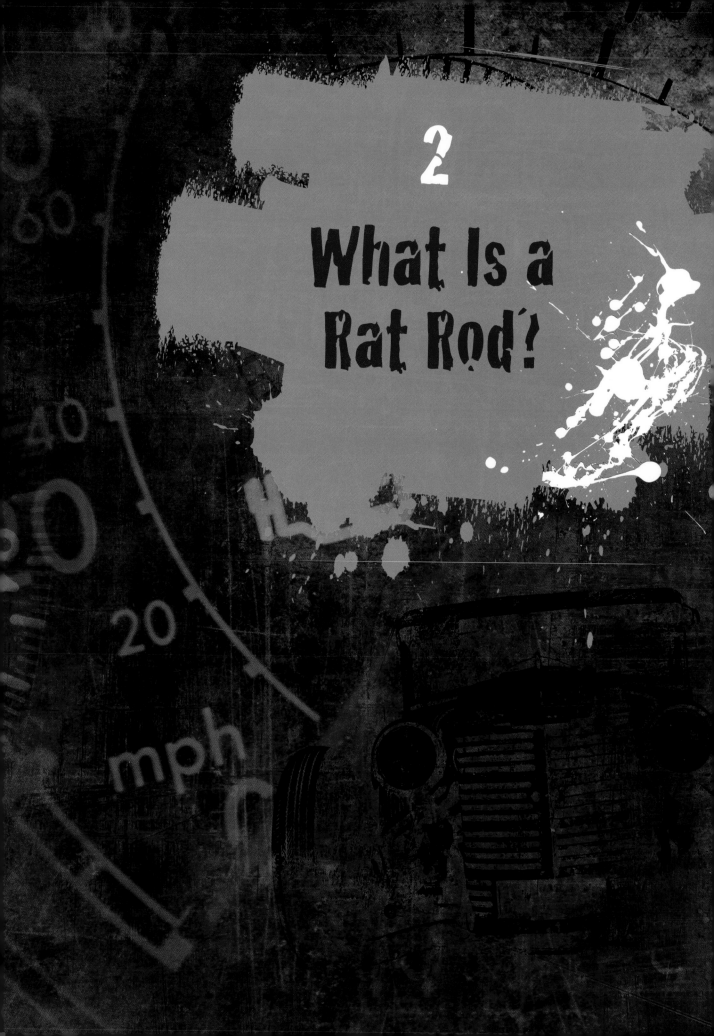

We've traced the roots of rat rod culture back to the beginning of the automobile: from the doodlebug to the jalopy and all the way to the hot rod scene of the 1960s. But where does today's rat rod really come from? The rat rod scene has continued to evolve and has taken on a life of its own in the twenty-first century. Today's rat rod pays homage to the hot rod of old while bringing its own modern ingenuity and style to the table. Its charm lies in its vintage appeal and its rebellious nature.

Many different sources have claimed to have coined the term "rat rod" or have tried to pin its first usage to a certain person, publication, or club. The fact of the matter is that no one truly knows when the term was first used, how it was first used, or who used it first.

In this book, we won't even try to track the term's origins because that effort would be based on unverifiable resources and ultimately would result in more speculation. The early history of the term itself will remain mysterious and debatable until someone develops time travel and we can go back and figure it all out.

For the sake of factual explanation of the history of rat rod culture, we will emphatically declare that the term "rat rod" has its own unique meaning today and that wherever it originated is irrelevant. Because the term is so polarizing, and because what exactly a rat rod is or isn't has been such a hot topic, let's delve into a couple of previously published articles from *Rat Rod Magazine*.

Spectators enjoy the rat rods on display at the annual Lonestar Roundup event in Austin, Texas.

An Open Letter from the Editor

What Is a Rat Rod?

Published in *Rat Rod* in January 2011, this article was the magazine's first official response to the question of "what is a rat rod?"

Before I dig into this question, let me start off with a little disclaimer: I appreciate all cars. I'm not a hater. If you're into shiny restorations or European sports cars, so be it. I don't understand why people get so bent out of shape about someone else's tastes … I mean, a little harmless chiding is no big deal, but I've seen some pretty aggressive arguments over what kind of car scene someone is into. I myself grew up in a racing family. My dad was racing stock cars from the day I was born, so I grew accustomed to watching him slave away in the garage, trying to get the car ready for the weekends. I've always had a love for the classics, especially American muscle, and an appreciation for anything that looks cool or goes fast. But, yes, I do like rat rods the most, and I've developed a healthy respect for them and their builders. If you hate rats, you probably shouldn't be reading a copy of *Rat Rod Magazine*. As a rat rod guy, and the editor of this magazine, I feel obligated to at least share my opinion with you about what I personally feel that a rat rod is. The truth of the matter is, you can ask ten different people, and they will all give you a different answer. There are a lot of people out there who will tell you matter-of-factly that a rat rod is (whatever they think it is), and some will even tell you exactly where the term originated … some folks have even tried to take credit for creating the term. Internet research will ultimately bring you to a couple of different common definitions. From *Wikipedia*: "A rat rod is a style of hot rod or custom car that, in most cases, imitates (or exaggerates) the early hot rods of the '40s, '50s, and '60s. It is not to be confused with the somewhat closely related 'traditional' hot rod, which is an accurate recreation or period-correct restoration of a hot rod from the same era."

Rat rods have been aptly described as "rough around the edges."

Or how 'bout this definition from Fat Tony at RatRodStuff.com: "A rat rod is simply a custom car that is made for driving and hanging out with friends. Rat rods aren't ultra-glossy show cars. Instead, a rat rod is an 'unfinished' street rod that is intentionally left a bit rough around the edges." Here's one from streetrods-online.com: "A rat rod is a newly developed name for the original hot rod style of the early 1950s. A rat rod is usually a vehicle that has had many of its non-critical parts removed. They are usually finished in primer or paints that are often period-correct. They are very often a conglomeration of parts and pieces of different makes, models, and aftermarket parts. The term 'rat rod' was first used by the high-dollar, show-car guys to describe the low-buck, home-built drivers. Don't forget the roots of the hobby (street rods); it was the little guy in a garage on a budget (with help from his friends) that started it all." Then there's the squidoo.com definition: "A rat rod is an older car or truck that's still roadworthy but has been stripped down to basics and then rebuilt (usually) with accessories and parts that date approximately from the same period as the original car."

Using old truck bodies for builds is popular among rat-rod enthusiasts.

You get the idea. There are definitely some points that just about everyone agrees on, and then we have this massive gray area full of opinions and ideas that can range from traditional thinking to overly creative conceptualism. For the record: this magazine is a product of the entire rat rod scene, from every angle, covering all personalities, ideals, and components. What it really comes down to is the fact that a rat rod can be whatever you want it to be. You might be laughed at for building something goofy or praised for stretching the boundaries. There is a fine line between ridicule and respect, at least in the world of hot rods. The rat rod scene seems to be more accepting, more free-spirited, more rebellious, and more open to individual interpretation. My observation is this—if someone says, "Hey, you can't do that!," someone's gonna do it.

The rat rod culture is more than just building Frankenstein's ride or a flat black hot rod—it is about that rebellious blue-collar attitude that counteracts the sparkly high-dollar hot rod scene. Where the term "rat rod" really came from is up for debate, but the rat rod mentality has been around since people started modifying, piecing together, and showcasing cars. Wherever there is a high-dollar hobby or movement, you can bet your butt that there will be a counterculture movement representing "the other folks." So, let me get to the point here and try to explain what I think a rat rod is and isn't. Flat black paint alone does not make it a rat rod. I know popular belief would say that if it's flat black, it's a rat rod … but I beg to differ. Sure, many rats are flat black or painted in primer. I do believe that a rat rod can also be shiny. A rat can have a nice coat of paint, clear coat, some chrome—fine. Having those things doesn't immediately rule it out in my eyes. You have to look at the whole picture. Your rat rod doesn't have to have a rat drawing, the words "rat rod" airbrushed on it, or a toy rat zip-tied to the dip stick to be a rat rod. I know, if you've got one, you want people to understand that *yes, this is a rat rod*. But there's a point where it can become too much, and, in my opinion, if you have to *tell* people that it's a rat, it might not be one. Now, I have seen some cool rats with toy rats on them and the words "rat rod" stuck all over, and they looked good, but I am more and more turned off by the blatant "look at me" rat decoration. Trust me, if your rat is cool, there is no need for decoration. Patina is *awesome*. I love rust, decay, age, and distressed steel. Patina is a beautiful, natural part of decay. A natural rusty patina is like war paint over battle scars and the remnants of a storied past. Patina is something that

Rat rods wear their rust with pride.

can't be reproduced (or reproduced well). Time-worn parts paired with cool road-warriorish modern machinery is mixing past and present for a new level of cool. This is the essence of rat rod creativity.

Mechanical creativity can be downright diabolical. A rat rod in my eyes should be a mixture of mechanical things. Different makes and models, parts from different eras, junkyard collectibles. Part of the rat rodder's credo is the "use what you got" mentality. Rat rod creativity should never just be on the surface—it should be internal, as a whole. Show me an engine in a car that it was never meant to be in; show me a car built from scavenged parts; show me what you can do with a pile of rusty steel that's been rotting away in a farmer's field for fifty years; show me a car that looks like a monster but drives like a cheetah. Build it, don't buy it. Look, I've got nothing against the guy who buys cool stuff for his rat, but anybody with some cash can do that. Get your hands dirty! I'm always amazed by the amount of work that can go into a car, and oftentimes I'm blown away by what people can do, especially with limited resources. I have a ton of respect for a guy who locks himself in the garage for a winter and comes out in the spring with something that'll kick some serious butt and look cool doing it. Most importantly: *drive it.* Anything built (or bought) to be hauled around on a trailer isn't a vehicle, it's a trophy, a showpiece. I love looking at restored classics, muscle cars, race cars, antiques—I love all of that stuff, and they have their place in automotive history. However, rat rods are not meant to be hauled. I won't even put a car in this magazine if it's not used. Rats are really meat-and-potato machines. I need to see bugs in the radiator and burnt rubber on the quarter panels. They should be mean and gritty and have plenty of attitude. Function over flavor, baby.

So what will or won't I feature in this magazine? After reading all of this, you pretty much know where I stand, but here's what really turns me on: cars and trucks that represent the rat rod culture. I'm looking for daily drivers. Rats that are built to DO something. Rats that are built by hand, in the backyard, in the local shop, in a rickety old garage. Rats built from salvage-yard treasures. Rats that are made from a bunch of different sources from different generations. Rats that have meaning behind their existence. Rats and owners/builders that have a story.

Creativity, both mechanical and aesthetic. Rust. Patina. Big steel balls to go along with big steel pipes, with engines that churn out thunderous fury, flame-blasting exhausts, and the smell of burnt high-octane fuel. This is my interpretation of what is and what is not a rat rod. I challenge everyone out there to form your own opinions and find your own "cool." Rat on!

—— **by Steve Thaemert**

I published the following letter in the June/July 2014 issue of *Rat Rod Magazine, also* in response to the what-is-a-rat rod debate. It sums up "rat rod" as a term, culture, and community. Only three years apart, these two articles share the same basic message.

Ratology,

an Editor's Letter

by Steve Thaemert, 2014

Four years after the birth of *Rat Rod Magazine*, the battle of *what is* and *what is not* a rat rod still rages on. Sometimes I wonder if it's just because people like to stir the pot … or maybe need something to argue about. Other times, they might genuinely want to know. Either way, someone is always asking "what is a rat rod?"

I've given my definition a bazillion times, and every once in a while I revisit the topic here in the magazine. I used to spend a stupid amount of time trying to explain my stance on what a rat rod is and how I have formulated that opinion, but it all comes down to this: *a rat rod is simply a blue-collar hot rod.*

You can spin off from that any way you want—talk about years, makes, components, paint, whatever—and it still comes down to that. I don't care who coined the term or when it was first used. This is what it is now. A rat rod is a blue-collar hot rod. *Period.* That is *fact*. It's not debatable. Everything beyond that? Open to interpretation, and that's what makes the rat rod scene so fun and inviting.

The fact of the matter is that a rat rod is the working-class answer to high-buck hot rods and street rods and all of the pageantry and ego that seem to go along with them. Rat rods are about heart, history, and having a good time. They're not about money, ego, and who has the most seamless clone of the car next to it. Rat rodders embrace imperfection, individuality, and the stories behind what they're building and driving. That's the beauty of the rat rod scene … you can create something that represents your personality down to every fine detail, and you can do it within *your* means. No one can tell you it's right or wrong.

I know there's a fine line between traditional hot rods and rats, and there's always going to be debate surrounding the use of newer vehicles and, many times, newer components—but that's OK. I see a whole lot of cool creations—rat or not—and they don't have to be labeled in order to be enjoyed. Someone will always be raising the bar and stirring the pot. So be it. Let's see your interpretation of cool, whatever you want to call it.

These are some of my own thoughts and opinions—take them how you want. The bottom line? In a cool sort of free-spirited way, rat rodding will define itself and always has.

Underneath the rust lies decades' worth of history.

Here are some other definitions from guys at

Rat Rod Magazine

To me, rat rods have been around for decades. I think they started back when people of all ages (mostly young) wanted a car and couldn't afford one, but they could build one out of parts that were cheap and easy to get. Most didn't have the money to put into customizing and appearance, so their efforts went into building a hopefully reliable car. I think "jalopies" were the first rat rods, so this is not new. The beauty of rat rods is that almost anything goes. Rust or rattle can, chopped or not, channeled or not, mixture of different makes and models. One thing that I don't think is a rat rod is a car with stuff welded onto it that serves no purpose and sprayed flat black.

–Craig Lankki, Merchandise Director

Blue collar, family-oriented, low-buck rod. Where self-expression can be explored and is encouraged. No rules to follow other than safety. An excellent entry into the car hobby. No belly-button or cookie-cutter cars; American ingenuity at its finest.

–Bryan Dagel, Head Builder

A rat rod is a car that's built with the sensibilities and basic style of the original pre-war hot rods with an eye toward creativity and personalization. Older cars with modern drivetrains and suspensions are welcome, separating the rat rods from the "traditional" rods, making the rat rods more accessible and achievable to the average guy or gal.

–Rick Loxton, Senior Writer

Rat rods are low-dollar, affordable hot rods. Just like back in the '50s, rat rods are the affordable cars pieced together with what you have or can afford to buy. They are loud, fast, obnoxious, and a blast to drive.

–Chad Truss, Staff Photographer

As you can see, even the people behind the magazine share different opinions, all based on the same basic principles but all slightly different at the same time. In 2015, I wrote an article describing what we were looking for to showcase in the magazine as submissions poured in from around the world. That's a good thing—unless, of course, you can run only eight to ten features in an issue and become severely backlogged with material. People began grumbling that we were rejecting their vehicles, which was really not the case. Could we or would we publish every rat rod out there? Of course not. But the majority of rat rods do meet our criteria for publication. The following excerpt from my article explains what we look for when considering submissions.

Plenty of legitimate rat rods are flat black, but paint (or lack thereof) is not the defining characteristic.

> The *Rat Rod Magazine* mission is — and has always been —
> to showcase rat rod culture and the builders behind the machines.

We're often asked how people can get their cars and trucks into the magazine, so I thought it would be a good time to answer in depth.

This magazine is powered by the rat rod community. We don't have any agendas other than to promote and support this group of builders and enthusiasts. It's important to us that *anyone* can get into this magazine, no matter how rich or poor, whether they're building in a shop or the backyard. If the vehicle represents rat rod culture and the build itself has merit, it has a shot in *Rat Rod*.

That being said, there are two common reasons a vehicle won't make it into the magazine:

1. we receive far more submissions than we can possibly publish, and
2. the vehicle or build just isn't rat rod relevant.

Now, we're not here to judge. That's important, because many times, when a vehicle doesn't make it into the magazine, the owner assumes that we don't like it. That's possible, of course, but not likely. We rarely "reject" anything based on our personal tastes. We *do* look at the build and the vehicle itself. Is it a rat rod? If not technically a rat rod, is it at least something that fits into rat rod culture? Is it built well? Is it safe?

The best way to show off a rat rod is to hit the road and drive it.

Our obligation not only to the rat rod community but also to the public as a whole is to stay true to what and who we are: and that is a RAT rod publication, first and foremost. We'll always capture some fringe elements, stories, and perhaps even vehicles that can't quite be labeled. But, we won't deviate from the foundation of this magazine, and that is *featuring rat rods and the builders behind them.*

The build itself is important. There are so many different building styles and methods out there, from a simple chassis swap to a full-blown ground-up creation and everything in between. We'll feature any build style as long as it's safe and represents the rat rod mentality in some capacity. Pulling panels off a car, manipulating them, and putting them back on does not constitute a build. That is a modification or customization—not a build. Same with throwing a rusty hood on a modern car—not a build, not a rat rod. There's nothing wrong with doing these things, but clearly that is not what *Rat Rod Magazine* is about. Does it have to be rusty? No. Can it be painted? Sure. Can it be a 1995 Toyota? No.

There's always a gray area surrounding rat rods, and we get it—we're right in the middle of that and are always talking about it. Because a rat rod is essentially a blue-collar hot rod, and that's what the heart of the rat rod community is building, that's what you're going to see in *Rat Rod Magazine*. I've said it myself many times over: the rat rod community defines what a rat rod is by what is being built and driven.

For instance, we've seen some killer '60s builds, even some utilizing substantial components from the '70s or newer, but if the bulk of the vehicle is too new, it's obviously straying from the heart of rat rodding, hot rodding, and all of the vintage charm that makes up these scenes. Too new, and it becomes a custom, kustom, derelict, modified, street rod, street machine—whatever you want to call it. But there is definitely a point where year matters and the vehicle can no longer legitimately be considered either a hot rod or rat rod. If you have a bad-ass 1970 Chevy truck that you've chopped, channeled, bagged, banged, whooped, welded, and twisted, more power to you. Our motto here has always been to build what you want and drive the hell out of it.

But just because it's cool, and maybe was built in the style of a rat rod, doesn't mean it's a rat rod. You wouldn't consider a 2000 Mustang with a Corvette engine, no front fenders, and a rusty paint job a rat rod, would you? No. Sure, it's using different makes and models and has some rust and, hell, could be chopped or whatever … but come on, let's get real here. The time of calling anything under the sun a rat rod is long gone, and the rat rod community has established what a true-blue rat rod is. It will always evolve, it will always change, but there will always be things at the root of rat rod culture that are definitive and absolute.

We love new parts. There is nothing wrong with using nice, new modern components—especially where safety is concerned, because, above all else, you want your ride to be drivable. Hell, many rat rodders are fabricating their own parts or finding ways to repurpose old parts and make them safer, stronger, better. That's the ingenuity that this scene is built on. But if your 1930 Model A becomes a 1995 Ford with a Model A title, you're in a whole different scene. The body and what a vehicle is titled as are very important. Aesthetics are important. If it smells, looks, and drives like a 1995 Ford, it probably is. If it's a Model A with a modern driveline, it's still a Model A (makes sense, right?).

A true Model A rat rod.

It comes down to this: *Rat Rod Magazine* will be featuring rat rod culture in whatever form it becomes. If it changes, we'll change with it—but because this scene is so rooted in nostalgia and vintage appeal, don't expect the scene to shift too far one way or the other. At the heart of rat rodding is a whole lot of history, tradition, and multigenerational involvement. As in the hot rod scene, the passion for these machines is usually passed down from father to son and so on, which means that the ideas behind it are always rooted in the generation before and the history that formed it.

This magazine exists to feature the blue-collar builder, the Average Joe, the common person, and so on. Your submissions, stories, creations, and passion are our foundation. Don't be afraid to show us what you've got! We're here to support and showcase this scene before anything else.

As I have stated in these articles—I am only one voice. The goal of the magazine is to represent rat rod culture in its entirety, as a community voice, and to showcase the men and women driving the scene with their builds. I can only hope that these articles and the other facts and opinions shared in this book can help to eliminate some of the gray areas surrounding rat rod culture and shed some light on the history of the scene.

The reality of today's rat rod community is this: most differences between rat rods and other automotive scenes are aesthetic. Paint, chrome, and other shiny new components are still often rejected by rat rod enthusiasts. If it's rusty, has patina, or is just an old survivor, it's likely to be called a rat rod at some point, by someone.

Rat Rod Magazine has featured many rat rods with paint. Maybe not nice paint, but they've had "newer" paint jobs (as opposed to the original weather-worn paint). We have featured rat rods with chrome pieces as well. No full-blown billet-laden street rods, but there have been touches of chrome here and there, mostly as accents.

Even these aesthetic elements that people reject are at least somewhat relevant in today's rat rod scene. It's best to look at the whole project—the build, components, historical significance—before determining if it is a rat rod or not.

3
Rat Rod Magazine and Other Media

In late 2009, in the midst of a recession, the rat rod landscape changed dramatically. Maybe the poor economy had something to do with it. Across the country, society seemed to be returning to its roots. Repurposing vintage things for modern use became a hot trend in everything from home décor to fashion, and rat rod culture was right in the mix. Once upon a time, thrift stores were places where people in need could get new clothes, dishes, or even toiletries. By 2009, those days were gone. Thrift stores and other vintage or flea-market-style businesses were flourishing. The thrill of the hunt and, ultimately, the discovery had become part of mainstream society. The automotive world had always embraced this swap-meet, scavenger-hunt, used-part marketplace mentality.

It was during the rather depressing winter of 2009–2010, when everyone seemed to be broke and anxious, that the idea of creating a magazine dedicated to rat rods and the people who build them first surfaced. At the time, I was working on some paintings of cars, something I did as a hobby. My father had challenged me to paint some rat rods because he had seen a couple that had blown his mind. While looking for pictures of rat rods online, I noticed that there was no print magazine dedicated to the scene, and there were hardly any full features on rat rods anywhere. When I did find something, it was usually in an online forum or through a Google image search. I

wanted something physical, with big, detailed imagery so I had a visual reference on which to base my paintings.

The fact of the matter was that there was nothing on newsstands that catered entirely to this community; the term "rat rod" was still considered somewhat derogatory and was certainly not widely accepted. Rat rods were very much judged by misperception and myth, and although the rat rod population was growing, it was still a fairly unknown part of the hot rod scene. The more I researched, the more I fell in love with rat rods and the community that surrounded them. I had an idea, and I called my dad. I asked him point-blank, "Hey, you want to start a magazine with me?"

Take the polarization of the term "rat rod" and add to it the public's unfamiliarity with the rat rod scene, the stereotypes, and the confusion, and you have the perfect recipe for failure. No one in their right mind would start a magazine (believed to be a shrinking industry to begin with) in the middle of a recession, featuring what many outside the rat rod community considered to be the lowest form of hot rod.

But, of course, it happened. My dad organized the event that would become the Princeton Swap Meet and Car Show so we could generate enough funds to print the

The 2011 Princeton Swap Meet was the second of these annual rat rod events to be held by the magazine.

first issue and also have a place to sell it. We were both struggling to find work as house painters (damn recession), and we were able to scrape together only enough money to print half a batch of the first issue. We sold those and rolled that money over to print the second batch and continued with short-run printing until we reached the newsstand.

The automotive world was in desperate need of a shake-up, especially on the national newsstand. With advertising dollars shrinking, and many of the large publications dependent on those dollars, life in print was changing fast. *Rat Rod Magazine*, though, would be built on people power, not on dollars. Sounds crazy, right? Well, it was. But if we've learned one thing from this journey, it's that you shouldn't underestimate the power of the blue-collar American.

In early 2010, we sat down to create the first issue of *Rat Rod Magazine*. With the photography of Chad Truss—who would later become a rat rod photography icon—some material from Ken Adkins, and help from a couple of photographer friends, we "learned" our way through the first issue. Between Chad and me, we created all of the content. It was printed, mistakenly using thick 100-pound cover paper throughout the entire magazine, making it extremely rigid and heavy. No one involved with the magazine was a publisher, which was apparent when flipping through Issue 1. Besides the heavy, thick pages, the pages were covered in large photos. Entire pages were dedicated to the smallest details, like a hood ornament or weld. These tiny details had been captured in the beautiful photography and then printed big. Definitely not the norm, as most magazines were more content-based with smaller photos. And ads? Nonexistent, really. That first issue may have had three or four ads, and it resulted in a very clean, visually stimulating layout.

The first issue wasn't perfect by any means; in fact, far from it. The page layout wasn't professional, and it lacked overall flow. But it was right for the moment, and off we went. We sold the first issue out of the back of an old 1950 International pickup at a car show. The magazine itself was an experiment.

That first issue sold out within two hours at a car show in the small town of Princeton, Minnesota, and everyone involved knew that the impossible might just be possible after all. While the print run was less than 1,500 copies, it was enough encouragement to push things forward. What had started out as a father-and-son project to simply provide a place to showcase the blue-collar rat rod builder was destined to become something much, much more powerful.

The magazine was never intended to become a business. Like its subject matter, the ideas behind the magazine were centered on giving the Average-Joe blue-collar builder a place to showcase his creations. Other magazines featured rat rods in small doses, but this was very different. This magazine was going to be community built, driven, and operated. No salaried staff, no big offices, no gimmicks. The magazine would be virtually advertisement-free and feature huge photographic spreads to show off the visual nature of these vehicles. Written content would be secondary, natural, and not overproduced. This was going to be as blue-collar as the cars within it.

The cover of *Rat Rod*'s very first issue.

It didn't take long for news of a new rat rod magazine to spread across the internet. This community was hungry for it, almost as if they were waiting for someone to finally cater to their scene. Although the first issue didn't challenge any of the other hot rod and custom-culture magazines on the market, by the time *Rat Rod* hit the newsstands, everyone had taken notice. The automotive publishing world is very territorial, and we were the new kids on the block.

Rat Rod Magazine didn't stir up just the automotive industry—it made a big splash in the publishing industry as well. In 2012, the Minnesota Magazine and Publishing Association (MMPA) awarded *Rat Rod* the prestigious Innovator Award for its new and creative approach. *Rat Rod* would also win again in 2014 and become the award's first two-time recipient. Between 2012 and 2014, the magazine won a total of seventeen MMPA Excellence Awards for everything from cover design to media kit. Not bad for a publication with one full-time staff member and a handful of unpaid volunteers.

A look inside a rat rod shows how much ingenuity goes into personalizing these low-dollar vehicles.

But, that's how it should be—the magazine that's showcasing the culture should live by the same principles that make rat rodding what it is. Low costs, hard work, honesty, resourcefulness, and creativity are all qualities that have helped make *Rat Rod Magazine* a rising star, even though its methods—and even its existence—go against the grain. This book is an objective look at the various components of rat rod culture, so we will save the behind-the-scenes stuff (wait for my autobiography for that!) and simply tell the story based on the facts. The fact of the matter is this: *Rat Rod Magazine* took the rat rod scene and stuck it right in the mainstream's face—and, on the other side of the coin, the rat rod culture embraced *Rat Rod Magazine* and made it theirs. It was a beautiful community-supported project that moved forward as one cohesive, people-powered entity.

Even today, this same relationship between the magazine and the community exists. *Rat Rod* still has just one full-time staffer and is still managed by volunteers. There are no lavish offices or showrooms— just an old basement, a couple of storage spaces, and the use of Bryan Dagel's northern-Minnesota shop. No fleet of Lexuses—our company cars are a few worn-out vans and, true to form, a couple of rat rods.

OPPOSITION AND SUPPORT

As news spread that we had launched a rat rod publication, submissions began pouring in from all over the country. And so did the hate mail. There was a negative sentiment out there among some other car-enthusiast groups; in certain circles, there were people who absolutely hated rat rods. Their reasons ranged from "rat rods are junk" to "rat rods are wasting valuable car bodies." And, of course, some of that was true at the time. Because the scene was so disorganized, there was a huge variety of building styles. People were calling everything from farm tractors to their flat-black 1990 Toyota Corollas "rat rods." The scene was a bit of a mess. On the other hand, though, there were some amazing true-blue rat rods out there that were well built, creative examples of American ingenuity in its purest form.

There was a point in the beginning of the magazine when the backlash got a little violent. The *Rat Rod* staff was receiving random threats and anonymous letters, all with the same message—we don't like rat rods or rat rodders, so keep away from our territory. Well, from a publishing perspective, we understood where they were coming from. *Rat Rod* was entering a space occupied by people and companies who had been doing this successfully for a very long time and weren't exactly open to competition or

change. Our unorthodox publishing approach—low ad ratio, low-buck vehicles, Average-Joe builders—somehow threatened the mainstream status quo, and those who felt threatened by our presence definitely let us know.

Although rat rodding was growing in popularity, not everyone appreciated this offshoot of hot rod culture.

There was even one letter in particular from an event coordinator (whose event went under) who really hated rat rods. In fact, in one letter to the magazine, he went so far as to share his dislike for people who wore black clothes. This letter threw out every stereotype under the sun, most of them absolutely ridiculous, showing the ignorance and naivety that existed toward the rat rod scene at the time. When I asked the letter's writer if I could share his letter with *Rat Rod Magazine* readers, he retreated and asked that it not be shared … and that was the last we heard from him.

The opposition was strong at first, but not unexpected. Automotive cliques and allegiances have been around forever, and those divisions are often generational. The rat rod scene's aversion to "rules" and perfection set it apart from other automotive scenes. Building a car with a mix of Ford, Chevy, and Dodge parts meant that purists from every bloodline could potentially have a problem with you. Keep in mind that in the hot rod and classic-car world, people were often striving for perfection, looking for that extra "bling" or expensive element to put them one notch above the next guy. Not everyone who's into shiny cars was like that, but many were—so the rat rod community and the shiny-car crowd both had some stereotypes to face.

Despite these challenges, the magazine rolled on, against the grain and to the delight of an overlooked community of talented builders and passionate enthusiasts. The rat rod community rallied around us, and we continued to immerse ourselves in the culture. We didn't just sit back and work on the magazine; we got out to as many events as possible, met with rat rodders, made phone calls, and talked to everyone we could within the rat rod community and even those outside it. Passion and drive took over, and we were all in.

Issue #6, the first issue of *Rat Rod* with nationwide availability.

It wasn't long before a national publishing company discovered the magazine and reached out to us. At this point, we had just released our second issue—only a few thousand copies—and were just about to print our third. That third issue became a newsstand "test" issue in a couple of states and was monitored by our publishing partners. When the magazine sold well—really well—we got the green light to take a shot at the national newsstand, for real this time.

By 2011, issue 6 of *Rat Rod Magazine* was available nationally, and, despite the grind to get it there, the magazine began picking up speed. Early print runs were in the 25,000-copy range, but it was a huge step forward for what had started only a year earlier in small-town Minnesota.

Whatever opposition existed died down considerably after the magazine gained

Issue #1's cover car, built by Zach Kurth.

national distribution. The blue-collar market, which is made up of the largest social population in the United States, was increasingly supportive of the magazine and rat rodding in general. As more rat rods were being built, more people were introduced to them at car shows and in public spaces, and the community of builders and enthusiasts grew by leaps and bounds. The more familiar the public got with the scene, the more the backlash faded. The magazine's success on the newsstand and in the mainstream market opened up doors for rat rodding in general and continued to push the scene into new channels.

MEDIA EXPOSURE

Almost simultaneously with the magazine launch, other outlets began picking up rat rod-related stories and content with greater frequency. Automotive magazines had always dabbled in the rat rod scene, some more deeply than others, but around 2010 there was a huge increase in rat rod "awareness," so to speak. As soon as the general public caught on to the craze, many media outlets could no longer look away. Early rat rod-specific programs, such as *Rat Rod TV*—a TV show that bounced around between a couple of networks and the Internet from 2010 to 2012—as well as online forums, groups, and video channels, led the charge as the rat rod scene exploded in popularity.

As *Rat Rod Magazine* continued to grow along with many of the other rat rod-centric media outlets, the scene became much more accepted. Rat rod events, which traditionally had opened their doors to all kinds of cars and trucks, grew in popularity. Some other events that had once stuck to strict guidelines—many even banning rat rods—began to loosen their restrictions, and rat rods began filtering into every event that welcomed them. Where there once had been only a handful of rat rod attendees were now many.

Early in this popularity explosion, when there were fewer rat rods at more mainstream events, crowds would bypass the expensive restored vehicles and gather around the rat rods. This caused a bit of tension but really added fuel to the fire of the rat rod scene. People began to realize that they could spend less time and money restoring these types of vehicles and more time driving and enjoying them— and that they were just as cool as the other cars.

As with many trends, TV is a huge propellant. Having a national magazine dedicated to the scene is one thing, but, in today's society, television exposure is king. Some of the larger networks have jumped into the rat rod craze.

The Discovery Channel, which has become known for its automotive programming, added *Vegas Rat Rods* to its lineup in 2014.

Vegas Rat Rods star Steve Darnell and one of his most aggressive rat rod builds, "Quit Your Bitchin," on the cover of *Rat Rod Magazine's* issue 26. In this issue, Steve shares what life is like trying to build cars while filming a TV show and how his main objective is to help grow the hot rod and rat rod scenes with the exposure from the show.

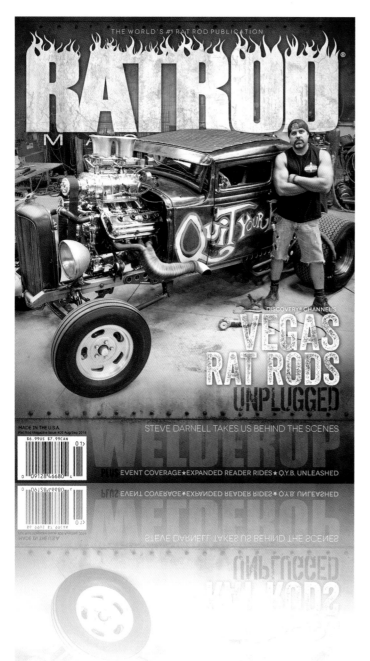

It features rat rod icon Steve Darnell and his shop, named Welderup, in downtown Las Vegas. Steve has built some of the world's most creative rat rods, and it was a huge boost to the community to have him appear on a popular cable network as the "poster child" of the rat rod scene. His extreme style of building is entertaining, and he builds well, always thinking about structural integrity, safety, and how much horsepower he can add to the car before it rips itself apart. Steve is a charismatic builder, and his team is personable and likable, resulting in a successful show that features rat rods and other vehicles being custom built for customers. At the time of writing, *Vegas Rat Rods* was filming its second season on Discovery.

Rat rods have been showcased on other national TV shows. For example, an episode of *Big Giant Swords*, also on Discovery, about a swordsmith on Martha's Vineyard who creates massive otherworldly weapons, featured *Rat Rod Magazine*'s head builder, Bryan Dagel and one of his Tour Rat builds. The episode also used clips from three of the Rat Rod Tours.

Rat rods have made many cameo appearances on everything from the History Channel's *American Pickers* to the various hot rod and custom-culture shows that have popped up across the United States and Canada. One such example is *Rebel Road*, which aired on the Discovery Channel in 2013. It featured several hot rod and rat rod builders as they geared up for a "rumble," or competitive car show, in Tennessee. Of course, the show was a bit manufactured, but the showcased cars and people were real—including Rooster McGee, who competed in the 2014 Rat Rod and Bike Build-Off.

American Pickers costar Danielle Colby with fellow picker and show creator Mike Wolfe's rat rod on the cover of *Rat Rod Magazine* issue 27. The rat rod scene and American Pickers share a lot of the same themes, including hunting for old relics and pieces of Americana and discovering the history behind each find.

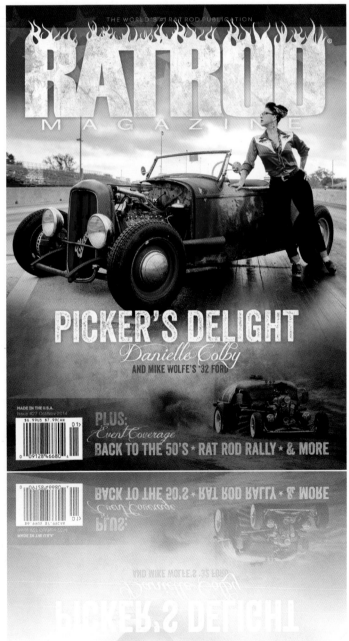

4
Events and Acceptance

ike anything dependent on spectators, most automotive events live and die by their subjects' popularity. While many car shows have continued to flourish for decades, many others have come and gone.

As rat rods became more common, naturally, more and more started to appear at car shows, where they became the center of attention. Their uniqueness, rusty and disheveled appearance, and often aggressive styling attracted a lot of interest. Love them or hate them, people had to take notice, and, in a sea of restorations and look-alikes, the rat rods were usually the most interesting exhibits. As with many trends, rat rods became the hot new alternative to the mainstream. They were an appealing change from the shiny high-buck cars that seemed to be everywhere, and they were inherently unique.

So what does a typical rat rod event look like? Take an event like the annual Redneck Rumble in Lebanon, Tennessee, which is put on by Both Barrels Promotions, a well-known promoter who coordinates multiple events throughout the year. It's been touted as the largest rat rod show on the planet, and it very well may be. Cars and vendor tents (and many campers) sprawl out across what seems like miles of groomed fairgrounds, all connected by an interwoven system of trails. As a spectator, you walk through literally a field of vehicles.

Clusters of buildings, such as restrooms, band shells, and permanent concession stands, are scattered across the grounds. It is a lot like a state fair or carnival but with cars, trucks, and bikes lining every possible path. Vendors are often set up in 10-by-10-foot tents, peddling their wares and showcasing their businesses. Swappers spread car parts, relics, antiques, and other odds and ends on blankets, across tables, in trailers— anywhere that they can display their goods. An event like the Rumble is a virtual treasure hunt for rat rodders, who never know what they might find while sifting through the scrap.

Typically, a rat rod show will start early in the morning, especially if there is a swap meet, because swappers like to have time to set up (and browse other swappers' goods before the spectators get a shot!). There always seems to be some sort of music in the air, and there's usually live entertainment, be it a band or a DJ. Many events hold pinup-girl contests or other activities to entertain attendees, with a final "award ceremony" to close the show. Car shows generally award car entries based on either a judging system

or a public vote. Part of the fun of attending car shows is casting your vote for your favorites—or your own car.

Where a more mainstream event might award shiny trophies, plaques, or other generic prizes, many rat rod shows feature handmade metal trophies or other original awards. It's common to see a table full of trophies sculpted from flywheels, brake rotors, spark plugs, camshafts, and any number of other metal or mechanical pieces. The trophies really do mirror the cars being awarded and further represent rat rod culture with their creativity.

Although there are usually awards at the end of each show, rat rodders tend to be less interested in "winning" things. When *Rat Rod Magazine* was first launched, many shows with which the magazine was involved did not give out awards. It was all about the experience, the fellowship, and just hanging out with fellow rat rodders.

Many events, like the Rumble or the Rat rod Rendezvous in northern Minnesota, offer weekend camping, which allows people from all over the country to attend the show

Minnesota's Rat Rod Rendezvous offers the spectacle of the cars with the comradery of the rat rod community.

without having to break the bank on hotel rooms. Having camping spaces available also allows for a deeper community experience, especially after hours, when people like to have bonfires, drink, eat, and generally have a good time.

At the larger rat rod shows, you'll also see a lot of smaller creative motorized vehicles. Mini-bikes and scooters are extremely popular, and so are nonmotorized offerings such as vintage bicycles. Customized rat rod-style wagons and strollers are also extremely popular; attendees often bring their children, and there can be a lot of ground to cover.

Overall, rat rod-oriented events aren't that much different from any other car show except that the rat rod atmosphere tends to be more interactive and participatory. What rat rodders often refer to as "shiner shows" get a bad rap because many a classic-car

owner will simply park his or her car, polish it or wipe it down, sit in a lawn chair next to the car for most of the day, waiting to see if he or she has won any awards, and then pack up and go home. Of course, this is a generalization, but you won't find the "sit-by-your-car-all-day" mentality at rat rod events.

Minnesota's Rat Rod Rendezvous 2010.

This drawing by hot rod artist Nick Sinclair illustrates the "no rat rods allowed" mentality that many events held in years past.

Another noticeable difference between rat rod shows and classic-car shows is that rat rodders welcome attendees to touch their vehicles. Many other auto enthusiasts give off a "don't-you-dare-touch-anything" vibe if spectators approach their cars too closely, but in the rat rod world, builders and owners welcome children and adults to sit in their cars, crank on the wheels, and have fun! Want to see what it's like to drive a chopped 1929 Model A with a blown hemi in it? Go ahead, kid, jump in. That attitude is very refreshing and has ultimately added to the appeal and growth of the rat rod scene.

Events come and go, sometimes because of interest, sometimes because of money or politics—but there are some that seem to live on forever. We've already mentioned the Redneck Rumble and the Rat Rod Rendezvous, but what else is out there for rat rodders? If you want a big taste of rat rod culture, check out some of the following favorites.

Rat Rod Magazine's Princeton Swap Meet and Car Show is held each year in May at the Princeton, Minnesota (Mille Lacs County), Fairgrounds and Speedway. The magazine started this event to help boost *Rat Rod*'s launch, so it has always been a "rat rod first" gathering. It's not the largest rat rod event on earth, but it is definitely full of everything that rat rod culture revolves around. There is a sprawling swap-meet and flea-market area, plenty of food vendors, live music, model and pinup contests, and, of course, fairgrounds filled with rat rods. It's an easygoing one-day event with a lot of entertainment.

Minnesota is also home to the largest classic-car show in the country, featuring more than 11,000 pre-1964 cars and trucks annually. Back to the '50s (BTTF), hosted by the Minnesota Street Rod Association (MSRA) and held at the Minnesota State Fairgrounds in St. Paul, is a must-see event for any car lover. This show has an atmosphere unlike any other. Hundreds and hundreds of vendors, dishing out everything from food to car parts, apply a year in advance to reserve space. Car and trucks—shiners and rat rods alike—line the streets of the fairgrounds for miles. The streets (yes, they are real streets, just like you'd find in any city, lined with sidewalks and grassy areas) are wide enough to allow a constant parade of cars and plenty of foot traffic between the cars. BTTF lasts for three days (Friday, Saturday, and Sunday of the twenty-fifth weekend of

Back to the '50s always draws large numbers of exhibitors and spectators.

The 11,000+ cars on display are only part of the entertainment that Back to the '50s offers attendees.

the year), and even if you attend for all three days, you can't possibly reach every part of the event. Put this one on your bucket list!

Minnesota seems to be a hotbed for automotive enthusiasts from a myriad of scenes, especially the hot rod and rat rod scenes. The long-running but now defunct Lowbrow High Octane event was staged downtown in historic Northfield and featured numerous live bands and an art gallery along with the car show. Other Minnesota events, such as the Rat Rod Rally in Sturgeon Lake, way up north, wows spectators with rat rod radar runs in which contestants run their cars down a dirt straightaway and try to reach the fastest speed. Throughout each summer, there are rat rod-friendly events at least twice a month in different Minnesota locations and with different themes and types of entertainment.

One Minnesota event that can't be overlooked is the Frankensteiners Ball, hosted by the Frankensteiners Car Club in Anoka at the fairgrounds each October. The Ball consistently attracts well over 1,000 cars and trucks of all types, not just rat rods and shiners. Begun in 2006, the event has a Halloween theme, and show-goers often dress in costumes and participate in the annual costume contest. Car owners decorate their rides in spooky treatments and hand out candy, and there is plenty of entertainment, earning the Ball a reputation as a family-friendly event. The other nice thing about the Ball and many of these other Minnesotan events is that they are open to all cars and trucks—not just rat rods, not just shiners.

Venturing out of Minnesota, more notable shows tend to follow the path of the Mississippi River south through the Midwest. Started in 2010, Shapiro Steelfest in St. Louis, Missouri, has quickly become one of the nation's most anticipated rat rod events. Hosted right in the middle of the Shapiro Metal Supply steelyard and compound, the event oozes industrial charm. Vehicles are packed into the oddly shaped spaces in between buildings, and sometimes inside the buildings, and spread out onto the busy public street outside the property. The highlight of the show is when the cars exit. Spectators line the street (and even stand in the middle) to watch each car roast its tires on its way out. Even people on their regular commutes will burn out when passing through this spectacle. It truly is something you won't see anywhere else and has made Steelfest a can't-miss event.

A homemade trophy in keeping with the theme of the Frankensteiners Ball.

People line the street to watch cars do burnouts as they exit Shapiro Steelfest.

Steelfest is one of the rat rod scene's must-attend annual events.

PARKING
FOR
SHAPIRO—
RAT ROD

Traveling farther south and into Louisiana, you'll meet a whole other brand of rat rodder. Rat rod icons Dennis "Crabdaddy" Landry and Ron Alexander and some of the craziest Cajuns you'll ever meet build powerful rat rods and put on a show everywhere they go. The folks down in the Deep South have a lot of character, and they know how to have fun. Many of the Cajun rat rodders tend to cram as much horsepower as they can into their rods' engines. If it can't burn the rubber clear off its tires, it's probably not a rat rod down in Louisiana.

Southern rat rodders host shows all over the place, and one of the most notable is Atomic Blast in Gulfport, Mississippi. The "Atomic Blast" is a portion of the event in which drivers position their cars in a circle and then simultaneously blow fire and smoke into the center of the circle. It's quite a sight, and it's always a crowd favorite. This same group of rat rodders also host the Swamp Stomp in southern Louisiana. Yet another entertaining spectacle created in the name of high-octane fun.

The "Atomic Blast" part of the event by the same name.

Swamp Stomp is all about rat rods, speed, and mud.

Another growing force in the rat rod world is Las Vegas, Nevada. Las Vegas has long been a hub for, well, just about everything, especially custom and classic cars. It is home to the crown jewel of the auto market's trade-show world (the SEMA show) as well as some of the most iconic car-related TV shows of all time. Years ago, most people would refer to Viva Las Vegas, a custom and classic car show complete with burlesque performances and a ton of other types of entertainment, as the big Las Vegas car event. However, the event was not particularly rat rod friendly because the organizers wanted to maintain a more period-correct, traditional classic and kustom event, and rat rods were often rejected for entry into the show. That rejection gave birth to the RatCity Rukkus, a car show on the same day and in the same city, founded by rat rodders who had been turned away from Viva Las Vegas. They created something open and welcoming, and it has become one of the top rat rod events in the country. It's safe to say that on that day in April every year in Las Vegas, there is a lot going on.

The annual RatCity Rukkus is Las Vegas's answer to a rat rod-friendly car show.

5
The Rat Rod Tour

One of the more groundbreaking moments for the rat rod scene came on the heels of the very first Rat Rod Tour in 2011. Not because a tour was a new idea, but because rat rods were, although growing in popularity, still considered "junk" and "undrivable" at the time. One step in overcoming these negative labels was to actually get out there and prove the detractors wrong.

The first official Rat Rod Tour was a test. *Rat Rod Magazine* had built its first flagship vehicle—a 1931 DeSoto-turned-pickup-truck with a 1960 Plymouth wagon bed, fins and all—with the explicit intent to drive it around the country. The car was a true budget build, with most of head builder Bryan Dagel's efforts focused on creating a durable, efficient machine. Bryan had just joined the magazine crew and was eager to push the envelope. He, along with navigator Brent Bonneville, would take the DeSoto on a trek from Minnesota down to Illinois, Missouri, and finally Tennessee before returning home. The caravan that jumped on the tour with them was relatively small, and the duo spent large chunks of the drive conquering roads alone, but with zero mechanical problems and a lot of memorable experiences, their adventure would set the stage for bigger tour plans. Among the first tour's highlights were visits to several shops and landmarks, including the world's largest ketchup bottle and the old LEMP Brewery building in St Louis.

The first Rat Rod Tour was very spontaneous. Bryan Dagel and Brent Bonneville headed out with a paper map and a rat rod full of gear.

By 2012, the rat rod scene had taken a major leap forward. Events were filling up with rat rods, the public was becoming more and more interested in the scene, magazines were selling, and more rat rods were being built. Still, there were circles of unrelenting detractors. The 2012 iteration of the Rat Rod Tour was something that would silence many of them.

Rat Rod Magazine built its second flagship vehicle, again with the sole purpose of driving the wheels off of it. The first tour had sparked interest within the rat rod community, and it was time to do something amazing and "up the ante." How about take a caravan to the summit of the Rocky Mountains? The idea was there … and it grew. In the summer of 2012, the plans were laid to take a caravan of rat rods from Mahtowa, Minnesota, to the summit of the Rockies, down into Las Vegas, across the desert, over the Hoover Dam, along Route 66, and all the way back up to Minnesota. It would be an epic 4,500-mile journey that would become a defining achievement for both the rat rod scene and the magazine.

No one really knew what to expect. The critics were saying it couldn't be done: that the air was too thin for carbureted engines, that it was too dangerous, that rat rods couldn't handle the climb, and on and on. The challenge was there. Man and machine versus nature. If nature could be conquered, so could the critics.

The first tour stopped at some very cool places, including the reportedly haunted LEMP Brewery building in St. Louis, Missouri.

No journey through the Midwest would be complete without the sight of wind power in action.

LEFT: The entire 2012 tour was captured on video, including the beautiful trek to the summit of the Rockies.

The tour went off without a hitch. There was only one breakdown, and it was resolved without any other complications. Rat rods climbed more than 12,000 feet into a landscape that truly looked like the top of the world, and rat rod culture triumphed. The entire journey was filmed and photographed from within the group. Members of the tour created a forty-eight-minute documentary, titled *Four Thousand Miles of Rust*, which soon made its way online and garnered close to 18,000 views on YouTube.

RIGHT: Halfway through the 2012 tour, *Rat Rod Magazine* and the Village at Lake Las Vegas teamed up to host a car show in the stunning resort community reminiscent of a Mediterranean village.

Slowly but surely, rat rod detractors faded away—and with them, many of the myths regarding safety, durability, and drivability. Rat rods could be durable. They could be driven anywhere. They were safe and a lot of fun. The 2012 tour proved this.

After tackling the Rocky Mountains, Route 66, the desert, the Midwest, Las Vegas, and the Hoover Dam, it was hard for the tour's planners to trump their achievements the following year. The 2013 tour covered less ground but was be a cross-country drive of a different kind with plenty of cool elements. The tour began at the ceremonial starting point: TJ's Country Corner in Mahtowa, Minnesota, and followed as much of historic Highway 61 as possible along the Mississippi River all the way to Louisiana. Large coordinated stops

Empty landscapes become meaningful as the tour passes through, connecting the past to the present in a spiritual way.

The passage through the Rockies took an entire day and was a life-changing experience for all involved.

Video footage from *Four Thousand Miles of Rust*, documentation of the 2012 tour.

in St. Louis and Memphis were planned to break up the route, which ultimately concluded at the Cajun Nationals car show in Alexandria, Louisiana. Although there were no mountains or deserts, the trip was epic in its own right.

Adding to the excitement was the addition of the first Rat-Hard Build-Off, a cooperative effort between *Rat Rod Magazine* and St. Louis-based *Ride Hard Magazine*. Build-offs were common in the automotive world, but most were among preselected builders with some sort of celebrity status building expensive motorcycles, cars, or whatever could be promoted on TV. These TV build-offs were often surrounded by manufactured drama and a lot of posturing. The same formula was used to exhaustion: contestants would build extravagant machines, load them onto trailers, and haul them to some location to be judged. The first Rat-Hard Build-Off was the exact opposite. Participants would have a $3,000 budget and thirty days, and they'd have to drive their machines across the country. And there were no cash prizes.

Another addition to the counterculture charm of the event was that contestants were chosen randomly. This was not an invitational in which the coordinators chose the most flamboyant, polarizing, or well-known competitors. Instead, the Rat-Hard Build-Off showcased the common builder. Everyone had a chance, whether building in a driveway, a garage, or a shop.

After a call for entries through both magazines, build-off coordinators filled a hat with the names of build-off hopefuls. Although the competition was open to two classes, rat rods and bikes, only rat rods made a showing. Ten competitors and some alternates were drawn; of those ten, eight finished their builds and six made it to the end.

The 2013 tour and the build-off were captured on film, and another Rat Rod Tour documentary was released, this time to a much broader audience. In the year since the previous tour, the rat rod scene had grown by leaps and bounds. A very obvious sign of this growth was online: the 2013 documentary was viewed close to 350,000

The drive through Utah was hot but absolutely beautiful.

An iconic stretch of Route 66 that travels through the mountains and into Laughlin, Nevada.

We're not sure if we were the first group of rat rods to cross the Hoover Dam, but it was an amazing experience either way.

Two of the 2013 tour participants fist-bump on the highway leading into Louisiana. Every road traveled by a group of rat rodders is special.

times on YouTube, and *Rat Rod Magazine*'s Facebook page gained more than 1 million followers in less than eight months. Much of that growth is attributed to the successful tours, build-off, and the grassroots outreach these events created. Getting out and interacting with different communities on a personal level proved to be very powerful. The tours have allowed the magazine, its staff, and other true-blue rat rodders from around the world to bring the scene that they are so passionate about into towns and neighborhoods where people might never have access to it. They get to see what it's all about up close, and that is a profound experience—for both those discovering it and those sharing it.

In 2014, the tour was shortened to accommodate a much larger build-off. The success of the first build-off attracted a whole new round of hopefuls, and, again, contestants were chosen at random. In 2014, however, bikes made a roaring comeback, and the two magazines hosted a full field of competitors in both classes, plus a second rat rod "open class" in which the rules were less restrictive and there was no time limit for builds other than showing up to the final judging with a working vehicle.

Following in the footsteps of 2013's build-off and tour, the 2014 iteration ran through St. Louis and stopped at Shapiro Metal Supply as part of the wildly popular Shapiro Steelfest event mentioned in Chapter 4—a car and bike show right in the heart of St Louis's industrial district. The tour then rolled into Chattanooga, Tennessee, and eventually ended

The tour rolled through the Tennessee countryside in 2014 behind Mason Dixon's build-off entry, nicknamed "The Code." The group presented Mason with the Pied Piper Award for his efforts in leading the group on this leg of the journey.

at one of the premier rat rod events in the country: the Redneck Rumble. This tour included an epic drive across the hills of Tennessee with a massive caravan of rat rods and bikes that made up the largest official Rat Rod Tour group to date.

Rat rod culture is all about driving and experiencing the machines—the soul of old steel meeting the soul of America's old roads. If that's not magical, I don't know what is. The tours opened up a vein, and on the back of the only rat rod-centered national newsstand publication in the world, the tours helped bring legitimacy and respect to the rat rod scene. The tours have inspired a sense of adventure in people and forged that nostalgic connection that ties cars and miles of meaningful travel together.

The introduction and perpetuation of the build-off has also inspired a whole new

Following the 2014 tour, I wrote a very heartfelt reflection on all of the tours thus far and the feelings they had inspired:

It's All about the Journey
2014 Rat Rod Tour,
by Steve Thaemert

When Bryan Dagel and Brent Bonneville took off in the '31 DeSoto Tour Rat back in 2011 on the very first Rat Rod Tour, it was an experiment. We asked ourselves, "Is this even possible?" While that first tour wasn't very big—a handful of participants and stops and a loose idea of what we were doing—it opened the door for what has become the tour today. In 2012, it was the Rockies, Route 66, Vegas, and a lot of miles. In 2013, it was Louisiana and the first build-off. This year, it was the Midwest, the Rumble, and our second build-off. The evolution of this thing is fun to watch, because no matter how hard we plan, it just kinda happens.

Each adventure is different. The run through the Rockies was nothing short of epic. It was a smaller caravan, taking on a huge challenge, going toe-to-toe (or tire-to-toe?) with Mother Nature. It was intimate and fulfilling, and it created a bond between all of us who were there to experience it. 2013 had a different feel. It was a larger caravan, and the build-off added an element of competition that we hadn't experienced before. In the end, our family grew. Everyone involved walked away with something. Even with the stress of the build-off, the tour was a success.

Fast-forward to 2014. Our initial plans to tour into Tulsa, Oklahoma, fell apart, and we had to reroute the entire thing. This, of course, was a blessing in disguise, as we ended up connecting two very cool events (Shapiro Steelfest and the Redneck Rumble) with some meaningful stops in between. The build-off took on an even more central role than last year, and the caravan got bigger. The participation got bigger. The exposure increased. This is all part of that evolution.

Like the tours before, 2014's offering had its share of highs and lows but ultimately was a very successful event. The worst things that happened were a couple of breakdowns and a bit of discombobulated travel, which of course led to some frustration, but by no means ruined the trip. Highlights included keeping a massive caravan together through the Tennessee countryside, visiting Coker Tire and Stacey David's headquarters, and enjoying some tourist attractions in St. Louis, Chattanooga, and Nashville.

And to think once again that this all started up at a little place called TJ's Country Corner in one of the smallest Minnesota towns I've ever been in.

I returned home a little beat up from this one, but with a whole new appreciation for what we're doing. The good, the bad—it's all part of the journey. Without the challenge, there would be no reward. Without the adventure, there would be no experience.

The impressive line of rat rods arrives in Lebanon, Tennessee, home of the Redneck Rumble and the grand finale of the Rat Rod Tour and Build-Off.

Before and after: Chris Walker started his 2013 entry with a rotted-out '57 Chevy carcass and turned it into the 2013 build-off winner.

extraordinary. By creating a platform for the Average Joe rat rod builder, a national spotlight can shine on anyone—rich or poor, old or young, West Coast to East Coast. The only limit is really that of each builder's imagination. The budget, the timeline, logging miles … these are all part of the fun. Yes, they are a challenge, but the challenge is what makes the whole thing work.

THE RAT ROD AND BIKE BUILD-OFF WINNERS

The winner of the first build-off, held in 2013, was Chris Walker from Stacy, Minnesota. He took an unrecognizable 1957 Chevy wagon carcass and turned it into an amazing rat rod. The judges' panel was blown away by his ingenuity and vision, especially after

Everyone loved Dennis Hom's 2013 runner-up, a well-built '34 Plymouth with plenty of interesting personal touches—including a pair of skeleton hands that appear to be holding the exhaust pipes.

Rat Rod and *Ride Hard* dual magazine covers featuring the 2013 build-off winners.

seeing what Chris had started with. The runner-up was Dennis Hom of Conroe, Texas, whose creative details wowed everyone who looked at his car. Chris and Dennis shared the covers of *Rat Rod Magazine* and *Ride Hard Magazine* on simultaneous issues (issue 22 of *Rat Rod* nationally.) This issue of *Rat Rod* ultimately earned the publication its second Innovator Award from the Minnesota Magazine and Publishers Association.

In 2014, Hood River, Oregon's Gary Fisher and Team Resurrected Rust took the top honors with their panel truck in a very close contest. On the bike side of the build-off, Mitchell, Nebraska's Jeremiah Gardner stole the show with his steampunk-styled masterpiece. Both winners shared the two simultaneous magazine covers again (*Rat Rod* 28 nationally and the final issue of *Ride Hard* locally in St. Louis).

This build-off and the shared coverage also marked the end of an era for *Ride Hard Magazine*. Through the friendship between the two magazines, an opportunity arose for *Ride Hard* editors Jerry and Tracy Ripley to embark on a new journey and create a brand-new motorcycle magazine dedicated to the home builder. They shuttered *Ride Hard* in late 2014, and the new magazine, *Raw Bike*, was born. It carried the spirit of *Ride Hard* with a new national newsstand presence.

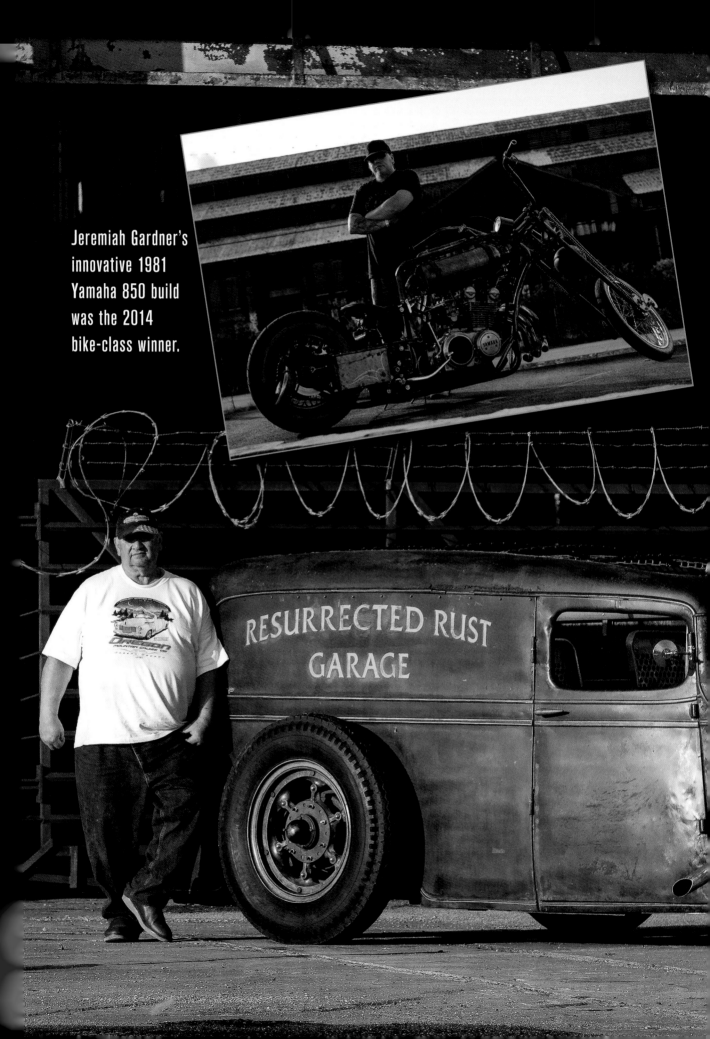

Jeremiah Gardner's innovative 1981 Yamaha 850 build was the 2014 bike-class winner.

RESURRECTED RUST GARAGE

The Resurrected Rust crew became the second build-off winners with their '33 Chevy entry, and they also traveled the farthest to compete: from Hood River, Oregon, to Lebanon, Tennessee.

6

The Future of
Rat Rodding

One of the magazine's flagship vehicles: the 2012 Tour Rat.

In 2014, *Rat Rod Magazine*'s media kit opened with the phrase "The new mainstream is here." The statement itself, although bold, was and is fairly accurate. By the end of 2014, the rat rod scene had completely dominated the hot rod market and infiltrated every corner of the United States. The high-dollar automotive hobbies continued their decline, resulting in the shuttering of many magazines and other media outlets. At the same time, more accessible, less expensive hobbies such as rat rodding grew to new heights. What was once a blue-collar niche market was becoming a widespread, fast-growing demographic.

We refer to the rat rod scene as a community, and it truly is. Like many automotive cultures, there is a common thread that binds everyone together. Maybe it's the tours, the hours on the road … or maybe it's the builds. The events. The comradery. Whatever it is, it's powerful, and it has fueled the growth of the rat rod scene as a people-driven, family-oriented experience.

A sense of adventure and fellowship has strengthened the rat rod community at its core and has inspired a multitude of spin-off tours, cruises, build-offs, events, and even publications. Rat rod culture has been showcased in books, in magazines, and on national television. It's been featured at some of the largest events and conventions in the world and has captured the imaginations of builders across the globe.

As rat rod excitement continues to spread, it will likely reach places we never thought possible. It has reached South Africa, France, Australia, New Zealand, and Sweden—all places where the American car bodies coveted for rat rod usage are rare. If people with limited access to that American steel can enjoy rat rodding, it's safe to say that anyone, anywhere, can. Even those who can't find American car bodies to work with are getting into the action—true to rat rod fashion—with whatever they can find. For some, a full-scale rat rod build isn't in their wheelhouse, and folks from all over the world are building scaled-down or alternative models. Rat rod-styled wagons, strollers, bicycles, boats, trailers, and even planes are all in play. If it's vintage, rusty, or distressed and can be given a rat rod treatment, it will be done.

It's no secret that there are only so many car and truck bodies from the 1930s, '40s, and '50s in existence. Eventually, even if it's many, many years from now, they will all be used up or discarded in one way or another. The fear that rat rod culture will plateau and then fade out when the car bodies are gone isn't entirely warranted because the ingenuity of the rat rod world will push its builders in new, unexplored directions. Already we are seeing people within the scene who are pushing the envelope. A good example is legendary rat rod builder and TV personality Steve Darnell and his extreme machines. Steve is known for his iconic "D rod," a diesel-powered sedan that has been the rat rod poster child for years.

Steve's aggressive building style is at one end of the rat rod spectrum, while others build with pure resourcefulness in mind. The opposite of Steve's extreme, powerful machines are the low-buck survivors and touring cars, much like the 2011 *Rat Rod Magazine* Tour Rat. Some rat rods are built to burn rubber (Steve's often fall into this category), and others are simply meant to be roadworthy. Some fit somewhere in the middle, and some are built way outside those lines.

The beauty of the rat rod scene is that there really are no limits. Rats come in all shapes and sizes, as you can see in this book. If you can dream it, you can probably build it. If it's vintage, low-dollar, or a patchwork piece of creativity, then it fits somewhere into rat rodding.

The future of rat rodding hopes to see continued growth of rat rod events.

PART III

THE FOUNDATIONS OF RAT RODDING

7

The Rat Rod Lifestyle

Part of the rat rod scene's charm is that it is made up of people from all walks of life. With a community this diverse, it's hard to pin a singular "style" to it, but there are some prominent lifestyle elements often associated with both the rat rod and hot rod scenes.

Rockabilly music and wardrobe are stereotypical of pretty much every classic automotive scene, but even more so in hot rod and rat rod circles. This style pays homage to the 1950s with its somewhat rebellious "rock-'n-roll-meets-country flavor," which fits seamlessly into classic-car culture. Many modern examples of rockabilly music have a more aggressive style with a punk edge, and attendees of entertainment-driven car shows and events often get to see and hear high-energy bands performing this type of music. While rockabilly may represent one side of hot rod and rat rod culture, anything that reflects the styles of the 1950s and '60s is fairly prominent.

Perhaps the most visual nostalgic tribute is the pinup girl. Pinups are everywhere from magazines to live events, and there is an entire hot rod subculture devoted to this art form. Anywhere there are people, there will be a way to celebrate beautiful women, and in the hot rod and rat rod cultures, this is certainly it. One of the cool things about the pinup scene is that it's more of a "girl-next-door" type of vibe that focuses on fun rather than perfection.

Another similar part of the culture that has its own subculture is burlesque. Burlesque is a style of performance that combines the sensual with the comedic; it is predominantly vintage in theme and traces its roots back to seventeenth-century Europe.

Vintage pinup-girl fashions and hairstyles are popular with many female rat rod enthusiasts.

Because the rat rod scene is essentially a hot rod counterculture, it carries with it a bit of an edgier contingency. While the rat rod scene is largely made up of "average Joe" blue-collar Americans, it does attract many "bad boy" characters. This rebellious nature goes hand in hand with vintage cars, although you can certainly be a clean-cut, khakis-wearing, tattoo-less rat rodder. You are, however, more likely going to see a lot of tattoos, jeans, t-shirts, and a general rock-star style at a rat rod event.

However, the beauty of rat rodding is that you don't have to be anything other than yourself, whoever or whatever that may be. Stereotypes? Yeah, they will always be there, but just as with any misunderstood (and maybe even a little mysterious) subculture, you'd be surprised at just how "normal" the people are. The rat rod community is made up of people just like you and me.

An often-overlooked fact about rat rod culture is how family-oriented it really is. It's made up of blue-collar America, after all—a segment of the population that generally has kids. At most mainstream car shows, kids are not going to be welcome to touch the cars, let alone climb inside them. At a rat rod event, attitudes are completely different. Because of their functional nature, rat rods are perfect for providing curious kiddos with hands-on experiences, and the cars' owners generally don't mind. In fact, rat rodders are more likely to encourage kids to jump into the driver's seat and touch things than they are to prevent them. Many rat rodders love to watch kids discovering these cool machines up close, in a way that they've probably never been able to before. In rat rod culture, it's a whole different world.

The rat rod scene is a melting pot of styles, ages, personalities, and tastes. Rat rodders come from all walks of life and are quick to express their individuality. The scene itself is as interesting as the cars, with so many different people sharing the same love of unique, bad-ass machines.

The rat rod community is welcoming to all types of people who are united by their love of the cars.

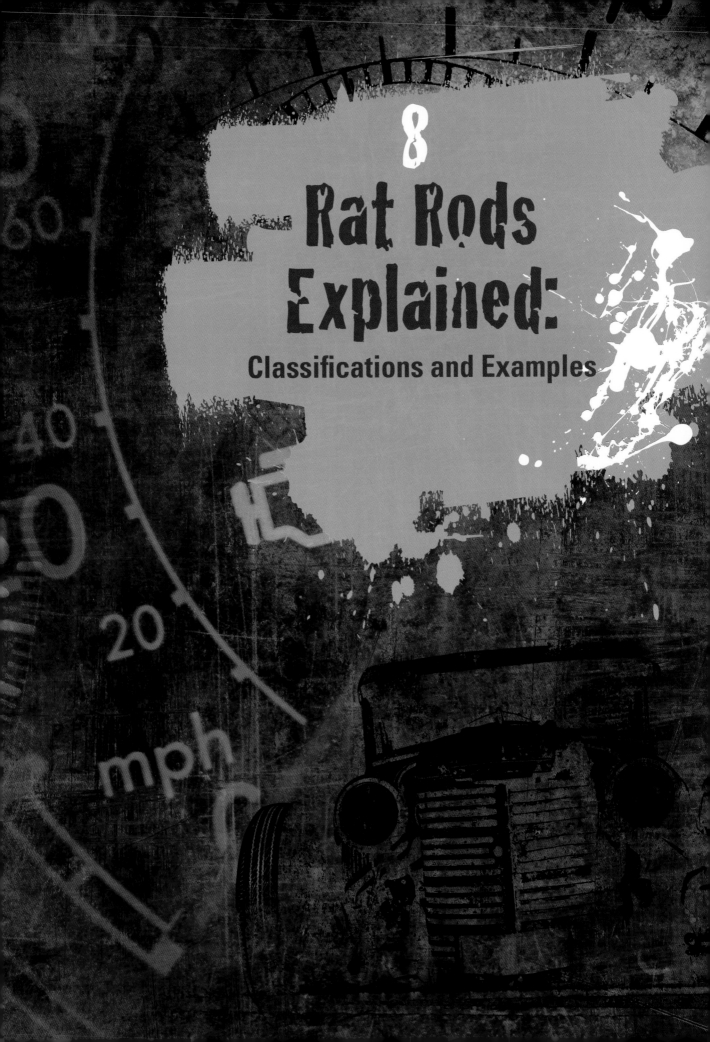

8
Rat Rods Explained:
Classifications and Examples

By now, you know that rat rods are, at a basic level, home-built, blue-collar vehicles. The point of building a rat rod is to create within your means, using stuff that's readily available. What may be easily available to or affordable for one builder may be completely unrealistic for another. And whereas some folks gravitate toward more traditional tastes, others dare to explore new paths. Part of the rat rod scene's appeal is the "no rules" attitude of the builds. Mixing a Dodge truck cab with a Chevy drivetrain and running a Ford engine is not only accepted but encouraged. However, for others, keeping things as close to the original as possible is the goal. Truth be told, the rat rod scene has something for everyone.

To better explain the "types" of rat rods, we'll break it down into simple categories. Most rat rods fall into either the prototypical category or the survivor category, but there are others that defy classification.

PROTOTYPICAL

As the name states, these builds pattern themselves after the original hot rods, gow jobs, and soup-ups of the prewar and immediate postwar era. Back then, as well as today, the scene was dominated by Ford simply because of the incredible volume of vehicles pumped out of Dearborn. But while the original hot rodders could cherry-pick the choice coupes, roadsters, and roadster pickups, rat rodders are happy to make do with the body styles and makes that the drag racers, hot rodders, and kustom builders tend to ignore. It doesn't mean that there aren't rat rod deuce coupes and deuce roadsters out there (there are, much to the chagrin of the mainstream hot rodders), but it does mean that there is a richer palette to choose from.

Nobody was building four-door hot rods thirty years ago, but since the price of two-doors has skyrocketed, they are now the norm. Those willing to put in the extra work can easily create a two-door from a sedan. All makes are fair game as well. Chryslers, Hudsons, Studebakers, and other previously "uncool" cars are welcomed right alongside the ever-present Chevys and Fords.

The increased popularity of trucks as a choice for daily transportation has influenced the number of builders who choose trucks as their starting points or even going as far as converting car bodies into truck cabs and then adding pickup beds from other vehicles. There's also a source of previously untapped raw material in the form of old cab-over-engine trucks (COEs) and heavy-duty 1- and 2-ton (and bigger!) commercial trucks that have never had a large-scale collector following. Cargo trucks, car haulers, tanker trucks, and more have been used as the basis of many very interesting rat rods.

One can argue that the overwhelming engine of choice is the ubiquitous small-block Chevrolet, specifically the 350-cubic-inch version. There isn't another engine with a greater combination of availability, low cost, and aftermarket support. Although there are rat rodders who maintain brand loyalty throughout their vehicles (Ford engine in a Ford body, Oldsmobile engine in an Oldsmobile body, and so on), the 350 Chevy can be found under the hood (if one is present) of every make under the sun.

A pair of prototypical rat rods built from 1929 Ford Model As.

Several other engines are popular among rat rod builders. The Chrysler Hemi, named for its hemispherical combustion chambers, is commonly used both for its reputation as a dragstrip terror and for its visual appeal. Both the early (1954–1958) and late (1966–1971) versions are popular, although the early version seems to pop up more often.

Buick's nailhead V-8, with its prodigious amounts of torque and super-aggressive cam, also harkens back to the days of early hot rodders. Another option for those choosing to go the nostalgia route is the Ford flathead V-8. While they don't make the power of an overhead valve engine, the "cool factor" is off the charts when one of these rumbles into a show. Those really daring to be different have employed a variety of straight sixes, not only for the freak factor but because their lack of desirability makes them bargains to purchase. As an added bonus, the light weight of most rat rods makes for a better horsepower-to-weight ratio.

Appearance-wise, rat rods further differentiate themselves from the hot rods of yore by the addition of more personal touches. The end result owes more to the imagination of the builder than to any particular credo. Design cues run from clever to kitschy, and, more often than not, they evoke some kind of reaction from fellow builders and spectators alike. Because of how deeply the love of automobiles is engrained in the American way of life, these creations become folk art.

BOB JOHNSON'S FRANKENKOUPE

 A perfect example of a prototypical rat rod is Bob Johnson's 1929 Model A coupe. "Frankenkoupe" was created much like the name suggests: everything was scavenged from the remains of recently (and not-so-recently) departed vehicles. In fact, Bob started out with little more than a set of quarter panels and a tail pan.

Bob Johnson's "Frankenkoupe" started with the body of a 1929 Model A. Inset: A look at Frankenkoupe's interior and Bob's personal touches.

The body is a basic 1929 Model A coupe, with a roof fabricated from a 1984 S-10 Blazer. The headlights are from a 1937 Studebaker. The chrome cowl scoop? From another orphan make—this time, a 1952 Packard. The taillights are 1949 Chrysler, and the third brake light is from a Dodge Power Wagon. Bob threw in a 5-inch chop and 3-inch channel job as well, and he made great use of a 1959 Chevy dash on the inside for a nice custom touch.

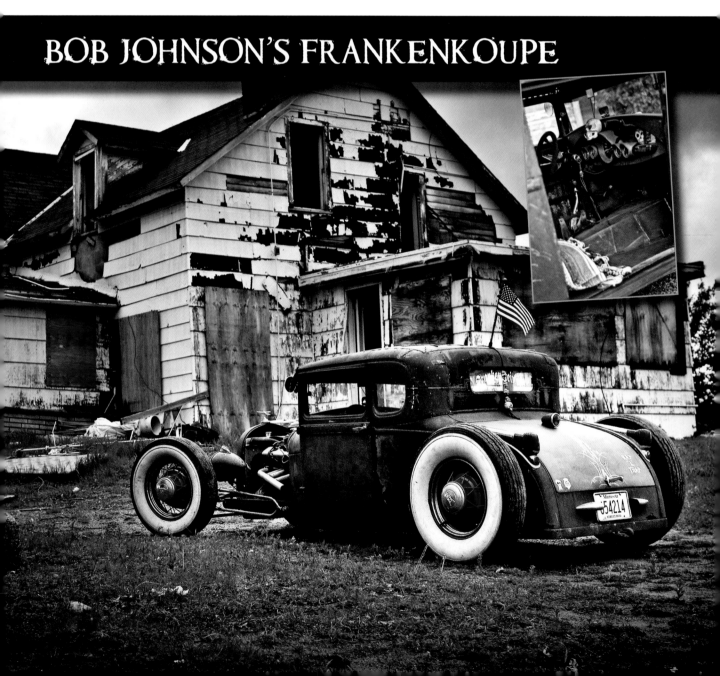

BOB JOHNSON'S FRANKENKOUPE

Frankenkoupe rides on a totally custom homebuilt frame that's Z'd 3 inches in the front and 14 inches in the rear. The front suspension is a drop axle with hairpins (as a fenderless rod should be!). The rear end is from an S-10 pickup, and the whole thing rolls on 1935 Ford wires shod with wide whites. The engine is a Chevy 350, while gear selection is provided by a Turbo 350.

RICK KUKKONEN'S MODEL A

Another prototypical rat rod is Rick Kukkonen's 1929 Model A sedan (no, not all prototypical rat rods are 1929 Model As; these two examples just happen to be very similar). Rick is a metalworker by trade, so his rat rod clearly showcases that skill set.

While not overbearing, copperwork highlights decorate much of the car. The car itself has a dark, almost menacing look to it, and the copper and custom leather details stand out. Rick's rat rod was actually one of the cars that first inspired the creation of *Rat Rod Magazine*.

Rick's Model A rod was part of the inspiration behind *Rat Rod Magazine*. Inset: An up-close look at some of Rick's custom touches.

RICK KUKKONEN'S MODEL A

PAIR OF ACES

This "Pair of Aces" was built by two friends out of 1929 Model As: one coupe and one sedan.

KEITH JOHNSON AND JEFF THRON'S PAIR OF ACES

In the rat rod world, Ford Model As are undoubtedly the most common cars out there. In this example, we have a pair of '29s built at the same time, in the same shop, over the course of about six months in 2009 by two friends, Keith Johnson and Jeff Thron, in Wisconsin.

When Keith and Jeff arrived to pick up the sedan that they had bought on eBay, it turned out that the seller had a Model A coupe body lying around as well. The men bought both bodies, and the builds began. Their goal was to have them running and driving for the Back to the '50s car show, which they just barely accomplished.

Keith, a mechanical designer by trade, got to work designing a frame. He drew up the frame using CAD software, printed out the blueprints, and started welding. Both cars have the same frame under them, and Keith and Jeff gathered the other parts as they were fabricating.

Powering the coupe is a 355-cid Chevy with a tri-power intake. The sedan has a 400-cid Chevy up front, also with a tri-power intake. Keith and Jeff sourced out TH350 transmissions for both cars.

They built the front suspensions with aftermarket lowered front beams, late 1930s spindles and wishbones, and they gave each car a disc-brake kit from Speedway. The rear suspensions, built in tandem, are four-link setups with panhard bars, and they used air suspension instead of springs and shocks. They sent power to the wheels through a Pontiac 10-bolt rear end on both cars; the only difference is that Keith's coupe has posi, and Jeff's sedan is a one-wheel wonder.

Keith hand-built the steering columns for both cars with ¾-inch tubing and flange bearings from the hardware store. Each column is topped off with a Superior 500 steering wheel: sparkling green in the coupe and wood in the sedan. Lokar shifters select the gears, and Autometer speedos keep tabs on how fast they are going. Keith went the comfort route and had some seats made by Stitch Bitch while Jeff claimed, "I don't need no stinking seats!"

BRAD BONNEVILLE'S THEE DEMON

Brad Bonneville's 1928 Ford two-door sedan called "Thee Demon" is another example of a prototypical rat rod. Although extremely unique, this car also exemplifies the spirit of rat rod culture aesthetically with its blue-collar build.

Brad Bonneville built a prototypical rod from a 1928 Ford two-door sedan.

BRAD BONNEVILLE'S THEE DEMON

While your typical rat rod is not normally festooned with firearms, Brad saw fit to incorporate a freebie Western Field 12-gauge into this build. The action has been welded shut to keep John Law happy, but it still looks the part. He also gave the body a good 6-inch chop and channeled it 3 inches. The doors were in such sorry shape that Brad just welded them shut and opened up the roof. The resulting hole was covered with the remnants of a 1976 Nova roof. That same '76 Nova gallantly donated its complete drivetrain as well—from the stock 250 six-banger to the equally stock Turbo 350 tranny, all the way back to the open ten-bolt rear.

BRUCE BROEKING'S MASH-UP

Bruce Broeking's patchwork masterpiece is an example of a rat rod that really is a mash-up of makes and models and has a lot of different influences. Bruce is a diehard Mopar guy, but his '34 Chevy pickup sports body panels from a Model A Ford, a motor from a '64 Chrysler, and a grille shell from a '36 International. How's that for automotive diversity?

Bruce Broeking's patchwork rat rod incorporates parts from multiple makes, models, and decades.

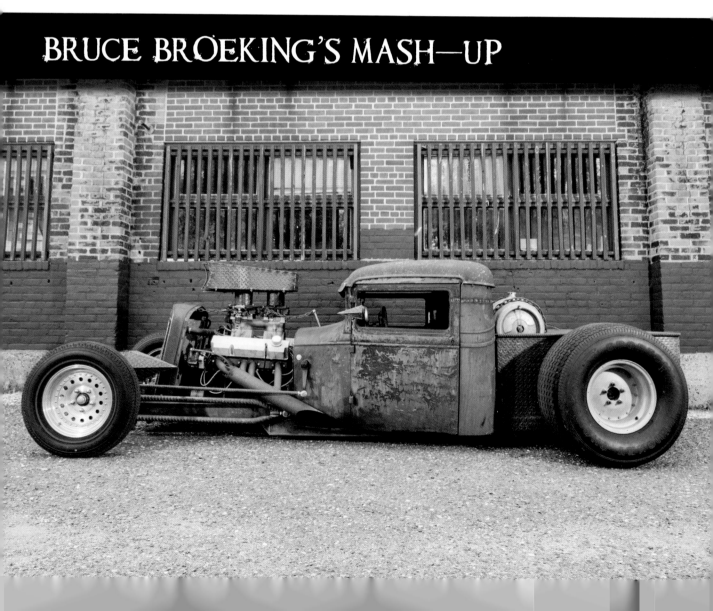

BRUCE BROEKING'S MASH—UP

He got the Chevy parts in true rat rodder fashion by pulling them off a rock pile in his neighbor's yard. "I think he still has almost every car he ever owned," says Bruce. The grille shell came off the same rock pile. The body wasn't complete, so he asked around to see what his friends and neighbors had lying around. It turned out that another neighbor had the Ford parts in the woods on his property. All he needed was a chainsaw to actually get the parts out of the woods. A few arboreal sacrifices later, and Bruce had the pieces he needed to make his body complete.

The body mods began with chopping the roof 4 inches and channeling the body another 6 inches. The original wooden body bracing had long since disintegrated, so Bruce engineered a more permanent solution by recreating the framework out of ¾-inch × 1½-inch square tubing, using spot welds where the factory had originally used screws. He used tread plate extensively throughout the truck, starting with the completely hand-fabbed box. It's also the material of choice for the handcrafted headlights, air cleaner box, and side mirrors. The taillights are repurposed 12-inch streetlamp amber arrows.

Turning to the motor, Bruce is running a 383 yanked from a '64 Chrysler Newport and added a Clay Smith mechanical lifter cam. He describes it as an "old-school type grind with lots of duration but not a lot of lift," and it gives the car that wicked sound. Crane cast-iron adjustable rockers complete the valvetrain mods.

Topping the motor is a tunnel ram featuring two center-squirt Holley 660s. The scratch-built headers terminate in the remnants of the driveshaft from the aforementioned '64 Chrysler. The horses are corralled into a bulletproof 727 tranny with a full manual valve body and set free through a Ford 9-inch with a 3.55 locker rear end.

The frame is home-brewed and constructed of 2- × 4-inch rectangular tubing. It's Z'd 6 inches in the rear and 4 inches in the front. The whole car sits about waist high to the average guy at the roof's highest point, is only about 2 ½ inches off the ground, and does not feature the use of airbags. In fact, the highest point of the whole car is the air cleaner housing!

The front suspension features trailing rods made from 1.5-inch diameter rebar. The cowl steering is also made from rebar. Suspension pieces rarely have stories behind them, but the front axle of Bruce's rat does. It's a mid-1930s Ford piece that spent thirty or so years under a trailer on his grandfather's farm. The trailer was no longer being used on the farm, so Bruce cut the axle out and added kingpins, brakes, and all of the other accoutrements needed to make it stop and steer again, and now it functions again more or less as the factory intended.

TODD MERTEN'S 1933 CHEVY

Todd Merten's wide 1933 Chevy is a great example of a low-buck but aggressively styled ride that exemplifies the rat rod spirit.

Drive north on Minnesota State Highway 169 until you almost hit Canada, and you will run straight into the city of Mountain Iron, which proudly proclaims itself to be the "Taconite Capital of the World." For those who don't know, taconite is low-grade iron ore that became much more important after World War II, when the higher grade iron supplies were exhausted. Some of that higher grade iron found its way into the 1933 Chevy coupe now owned by Mountain Iron's very own Todd Merten.

Todd is no stranger to this car because it has been in his family his whole life. When he was a child, he would play for hours in, on, and around the abandoned Chevy at his family's cabin. Years went by, and Todd forgot about the old Chevy because he was busy building muscle cars.

Turn the clock forward a few years to the twenty-first century. Todd was still crazy (about cars), but he suddenly had the itch to try something different. "I got tired of building shiny cars!" Hmmm…where have we heard that before? After going to a few car shows and seeing more and more rat rods, Todd got the itch and was soon jonesing to scratch it. He knew he wanted to build a rat rod out of something, but what?

Then he remembered the old Chevy. Todd had bought the family cabin after his father passed, and the car (or rather, what was left of it) was still there. While it wasn't exactly in pristine shape, there was more than enough there to work with, so he dragged it out of the woods and began his project.

Although Todd was new to the rat rod scene, he knew that many people based their builds on S-10 frames. Not that there's anything wrong with that, but Todd likes to do things a little differently. He had purchased a solid '85 Chevy C-10 pickup to fix up for his son. When his son decided that he wanted a car instead of a truck, Todd made the truck his parts source for the '33.

The first thing he did was whack the frame at the firewall. The stock 305 engine and Turbo 350 tranny were both working just fine and were never removed or otherwise disturbed during the entire build. The only addition was a set of Speedway headers with some tractor exhaust baffles to keep the noise down—but just a little. Todd built the rest of the frame himself.

The rack-and-pinion steering assembly is out of a Dodge Dakota pickup, but it wasn't always that way; Todd had initially installed a unit out of a late-model GM. He called over a bunch of his buddies to witness the maiden voyage of his '33, but when he fired it up, put it in gear, and cranked the wheel right, the car went left. "That ain't right" was the nugget of wisdom that came from his next-door neighbor. Todd still hasn't lived that one down.

Little did Todd know that this particular rack was originally firewall-mounted and worked opposite of how a normal rack functions. No big deal though—that's part of hot rodding. And speaking of steering, Todd's ride is kinda…wide. It's almost 9 feet across those humongous Mickey Thompsons. The car was a handful to steer until Todd moved the front wheels out to the centerline of the rears.

Todd Merten built this aggressively styled prototypical rod from a 1933 Chevy owned by his family for generations.

It's that wide stance that almost got Todd into a little hot water with the local police. He was out for a cruise when he was pulled over by the sheriff's department because his '33 takes up nearly an entire lane. The officer was about to question him about the legality of such a wide vehicle when he recognized that the driver was Todd—a good friend of his! After chatting for a few minutes, Todd was let off without so much as a warning.

The body has been chopped 4 inches and lowered 6 inches over the frame. This kept the rear window level with the rest of the windows on the car, which made the body proportions just right. The use of the C-10 frame versus the smaller S-10 frame is evident when you look at the exaggerated height of the engine. This, combined with the body mods and gigantic meats in the rear, give Todd's car a toy-like appearance. A big, mean, nasty toy, that is.

A peek into the interior will give you an eyeful of vintage cheesecake. The door panels are peppered with covers of 1950s girlie magazines. The driver and passenger are surrounded in relative comfort in the form of two padded forklift seats that were flipped around and tilted 90 degrees for a better fit under the chopped top. Each seat is topped with a fancy headrest from "some '60s Mopar," per Todd. A vintage foam-grip steering wheel keeps the thing pointed in the right direction. Todd uses a demolition-derby trophy that his uncle won in 1967 to shift gears.

DALE RAGAN'S MODEL A

Dale Ragan's Cadi-powered beast is an absolute work of art—an amazing machine that perfectly captures the rat rod spirit. Dale is all about speed, and the 500-cubic-inch, big-block, nitrous-injected Cadillac powering his 1929 Model A coupe shouts that out loud and clear.

Dale is an ex-Cadillac technician, so he went to his roots for an engine and sourced one from a 1970 Cadillac Eldorado. He tore it down completely and added tons of high-performance goodies. Inside the beast are hypereutectic forged pistons, forged rods, an SS plus camshaft, and Stage 3 roller rockers. Dale bolted up pro comp heads with fully ported chambers and also included a Cloyes adjustable cam timing set. Up on top of the big block is a maximum-torque specialty intake manifold and two 450 CFM carburetors.

Once the engine was all bolted up, Dale had his friend Chris Bathke plumb in the nitrous. On the dyno, this engine makes 520 hp alone and 809 hp on the nitrous. All of that power goes through a TH400 transmission with a Lokar shifter and a stall converter. An aluminum radiator by Dillon Radiators keeps everything cool.

Dale Ragan's Cadillac-powered 1929 Model A coupe.

The interior of Dale's rod harkens back to mismatched builds of his dirt-racing days.

The big-block Cadillac engine gives this rod speed and power.

Dale used salvaged gauges from a World War II aircraft.

The frame was welded up by Brian Helmintoler, and Lefthander Chassis did the three-link rear suspension. Dale bolted up the original Model A front suspension and added Speedway's 37-48 juice drum brake kit. He added a Franklin quick-change rear axle with a 4:56 ring and pinion.

Dale's Model A rolls on Coker tires. The front wheels are also from Coker, and the rear wheels are from Lefthander Chassis. Dale painted the wheels a copper color to go with the rusty body.

Inside this high-powered Model A are Speedway seats and a custom fabricated and pinstriped driveshaft tunnel. The gauges are out of a World War II airplane and feature a knots speed gauge, attacking angle gauge, and landing gear gauges.

Dale loves rat rods because they remind him of his dirt-racing days in the 1960s, when he and his friends salvaged all of their parts from each other and the salvage yards. They mismatched any components they could find and pieced their cars together with no paint, just a number painted on the door.

EXTREME

While rat rods are the choice of the budget-minded builder, bear in mind that different people have different budgets. We've seen $800 builds capable of driving back and forth across the country, but we've also seen vehicles that feature tens of thousands of dollars' worth of parts that were "just laying around the shop" and that took hundreds upon hundreds of man-hours to build. Nothing is off-limits when it comes to building these radical machines. Intricate, race-inspired suspensions help vehicles handle in ways that the original manufacturer never intended. Engines range from solidly built stock engines to aluminum-crate engines.

Full disclosure—some of these rides are built as show cars, where drivability takes a back seat to crowd appeal, but these are by far the exception to the rule in the rat rodding world. Rat rods are overwhelmingly built to be driven. Others are built to be driven sparingly. Three miles per gallon with a nine-gallon tank is not conducive to cross-country trips, but it is conducive to drag racing and burnouts. A previously overlooked choice that has caught on is the diesel engine. While nothing can replace the sound of a properly built V-8, a rowdy diesel has quite the ear appeal. The inevitable black cloud that follows the matting of the gas pedal in a diesel further serves to mark its territory. The other benefit of a diesel is torque. Great gobs of noisy, tire-frying torque. Perfect for burnouts, donuts, and drag racing, all while returning acceptable gas mileage and bulletproof reliability. But no matter how much money, time, and effort go into the mechanical bits of the vehicle, it's critical to any true rat rodder to leave the body as original as possible.

CHRIS WALKER'S 1937 DODGE

Chris Walker's 1937 Dodge tanker truck is a prime example of a rat rod that is on the extreme side. The motor is a Dart block with Dart aluminum heads. The pistons are 8.5:1 custom-made jobs, as is the cam. The blower normally runs 9 pounds of boost on 91 pump gas. When it's time to get down, a pulley swap takes the boost up to 13 pounds on 105 octane. All of this runs through a stout TH350 and the 8¾ inch Mopar rear with a ratcheting locker that came with the truck as purchased. How much horsepower is all of this? Only about 660 at the flywheel and 530 at the wheels, making this a true-blue extreme rat rod.

Chris Walker, 2013 build-off champion, turned a 1937 Dodge tanker truck into this extreme machine.

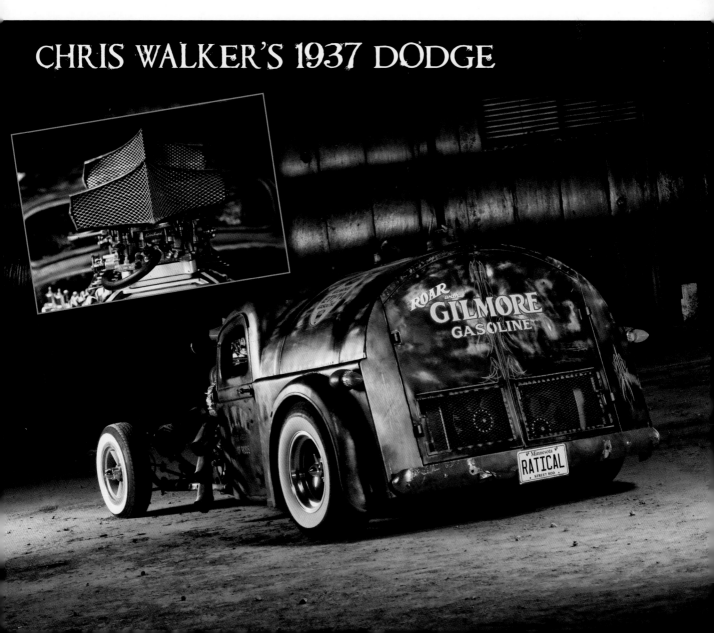

CHRIS WALKER'S 1937 DODGE

STEVE DARNELL'S QYB

Another extreme rat rod is the famous Steve Darnell creation "Quit Your Bitchin'," which has adorned the cover of *Rat Rod Magazine*. This monstrosity was shot for the cover of *Rat Rod*'s issue 26 by Dale Wigget.

When asked about this car for the *Rat Rod* feature, Steve had this to say:

"Quit Your Bitchin' basically was built for my brother, but I really wanted to build it for myself. What this is, is a big ol' 'shut your f***ing mouth' about what I build. I don't give a s*** if you build a rat rod, a street rod, an off-road truck, a mini-bike, Lincoln Logs, Legos … I don't care what you build. Shut your f***ing mouth and build what you want, and I'll build what I want. This whole thing is basically structured around four tires— that's it. That's how simple it is. We all are trying to figure out how to go down the road on four round tires. Just build what you want and go have fun.

"How can you go wrong with QYB? It's rat roddish and it has a straight front axle, a quick-change rear, a turbo 400 trans, and a supercharged 354 hemi, all in a five-window

Steve Darnell, creator of Quit Your Bitchin', is the force behind the famed Welderup shop featured on Discovery Channel's *Vegas Rat Rods*.

STEVE DARNELL'S QYB

Ford. You cannot bitch about that car. That pretty much covers everything. There's just nothing to bitch about. It was built in fourteen days, and it was a sh*tload of work. It was a completely fabbed frame. We spent hours welding, building, and redoing. The motor was in pieces, and we built that motor in three days. We had to cut the bellhousing of the tranny to adapt it to the 354. It's my vision of kind of a Rat Fink-ish gasser. And it's just really a cool car. We didn't have time to order seats, but in the parking lot we had a 30-gallon aluminum fuel tank from a semi. We cut it diagonally and made the seats. Those are the things that we do as rat rodders that save money. That saved me about $300–$400 on seats. My front axle and wheels were all laying around my shop.

"The motor is a '56 354 Chrysler Hemi with a 6-71 B & M blower with two 750 Holleys. It's an 8:1 motor. The bottom end is not full race and nothing really super crazy. It's probably at 600 horses. She's pretty dependable. The tranny is a Turbo 400 that came straight out of the D rod. [Author's note: We featured Steve's D rod in *Rat Rod* issue 13.] The rear is a late-model dirt-track quick-change all-aluminum tube axle. We made the rear wheels. They came with the ring and the center, and I wanted to make sure my offset was right. We ordered them with the centers out of them, and then we welded them in. We fit it to the car. We didn't have time to shorten the rear end or anything like that.

"The front axle is a stock '30 Ford that I had laying around. We put Wilwood brakes all the way around on it. The five-slot mags in the front are ones that I had laying around for years. The tires on the back are used ones I had laying around, too. The front tires are actually implement tires, like off a tractor. The headlights are just cool. They were lights that, again, I just had laying around. I like big headlights. They give it such a 'bug' look… like if it had wings, it would get up and fly.

"The '32 grille shell that's on it is an original, and I've had it for a long time. Motor Mission-built radiator. The interior has a full roll cage and a Speedway steering column with a quick-release steering wheel. The rear-end gears are 3.55s because I didn't want it so low that it would be obnoxious to drive. I wanted to drive it 70 miles per hour if I wanted to. It goes right down the freeway. The frame is all 2-by-3-inch square tubing. It came in on a flatbed and we cut it up, built some gussets, and started creating the frame, and it turned out pretty good. There was a lot of work there in a short amount of time. I didn't go real crazy on the interior because I didn't want to take away from the nostalgia of a gasser.

"With QYB, I just wanted to build a big "f*** you" in your face. The car turned out really good. We wire-wheeled the car because it gives it a burnt look, and then we satin-cleared it and gave it an industrial look. Dan put the motor together and did a really good job. We all worked out asses off on that car."

That pretty much sums it up. Steve's an intense guy, and he doesn't hold back—and that intensity carries through right into his builds. Quit Your Bitchin' has enough of a rat rod tone to it to fit into the culture, but is still not 100% rat rod. It has some gasser, some street rod; it lives somewhere in that gray area. As Steve explained, it doesn't matter what you call it.

AUSTRIA'S SEPP WEINZETL

The best thing about rat rods is that just when you think you've seen it all, it's like the guys in Bachman Turner Overdrive so brilliantly stated: "You ain't seen nothin' yet!" Case in point is one Sepp Weinzetl from Gneisting, Austria. He and his friends are absolutely crazy about American cars. Many of them build and drive hot rods that would not look out of place at any car show here in the States. But Sepp's gone and done something really, really different.

"About two years ago, I looked at some car stuff on eBay here in Europe. There I found an engine I had never been thinking about to play with. It was a nine-cylinder aircraft engine. The guy who wanted to sell the engine had made a table out of it with glass on top. The next morning … I couldn't stop thinking about the engine and thought that it could be the thing for a really crazy car. Three days later, the engine was in my garage.

"The first thing I was thinking about was a truck cab for the vehicle. I thought a cab would be the best body because it's small and you can see much more of the frame, front and rear suspension, engine, etc. The second thing was the grille. It had to be a Terraplane grille from the [late] '30s—a must for me. I love those grilles! Now I had everything in my mind to build a crazy thing and put it together.

"Some weeks later, my friend Luici Becker (who owns a CNC machine shop) came to my garage, and I told him about my new project. We talked about how I could connect the engine to a tranny. After a while, he told me that he would help me build an adapter. In the meantime, I bought a '34 Ford pickup from my buddy Jason Pewitt in San Francisco. I asked him to find a '35–'37 pickup cab for me. He did a good job and, after a while, he found the '37 Ford pickup cab for me. I loved the great rust patina! He cut the cab into two halves and put it on the bed of the '34. At the same time, I found the '37 Hudson grille, also in California.

"After two months, the main parts for the star-engined vehicle arrived in my garage here in Europe. Unfortunately, my friend Luici had a lot of work, and it took about eight months before he could finish the tranny adapter. During this time, I couldn't do anything except collect parts for the vehicle. Then there was the big day when [Luici] came to me with the adapter. Now I had everything to start!

"I screwed a welded frame to the floor of my garage where I could fix all the parts. I tried to find the best-looking position of all of the main parts, and I welded the grille, engine, cab, and front and rear axle to the frame down on the floor. After that, I built the frame and connected all of the parts together. It sounds easy, but it took months.

"I had no idea how this engine worked or how to get it started. By chance, a hot rod guy came to my house and asked me about a Model A hood. Then he saw the aircraft engine, and he told me about his friend. 'He has the same engine on a frame ready to start. He can help you.' After a couple of weeks, the guy came to me and taught me how to start such an engine. He also gave me important information about radial aircraft engines. They are not really like common engines, where you turn a key and start it."

About that drivetrain: it's a nine-cylinder radial aircraft engine of Czechoslovakian lineage from the 1950s. Displacement is 625 cubic inches, and it puts out 400 Cold

The nine-cylinder aircraft engine is just one of the notable features of Sepp Weinzetl's 1937 Ford pickup rod.

AUSTRIA'S SEPP WEINZETL

War horsepower. There are two spark plugs per cylinder and twin magnetos to light the fires. A custom adapter fabricated by the aforementioned Luici "Mr. Superbrain" Becker connects the motor to a GM 700R4 transmission.

As if the engine alone doesn't make Sepp's creation stand out enough, the truck makes a statement with its overall design. He chopped the '37 Ford pickup cab about 4½ inches and narrowed the rear window about 2 inches. It's also been channeled 5 inches over the home-brewed frame. He added a splash of flash with a chromed '37 Ford passenger-car windshield surround. But what really pops is how those custom touches to the cab work with the modified '37 Hudson Terraplane grille. Add to that the inclusion of a genuine set of Edmunds and Jones torpedo-style headlights, and you have a car that will stand out at any show from Venice Beach to Vienna.

Lest you think that Sepp's hard work stops here, let it be known that there is a ton of effort below the waterline as well. The frame was designed and built entirely by Sepp. It's been boxed in both the front and the rear and has been Z'd 5 inches in front and 13 inches out back. OK ... so he did use the rear crossmember from a 1930 Model A.

Supporting things up front is a '31 Ford front axle with a 4-inch drop. You'll also find '40 Ford spindles, '31 Ford radius rods and leaf spring, "early Ford" spring perches and shackles, and '36 Plymouth lever shocks. I don't know why, either, but I think he knows what he's doing!

The rear suspension consists of '41 Lincoln axle bells, leaf spring, and radius rods. There's also a Halibrand 301 quick-change center section, 31-spline NASCAR axles, and, once again, '36 Plymouth lever shocks. The car sits on vintage Dunlop racing tires and 16-inch '35 Ford wires that have been custom-fitted to finned Buick brake drums on all four corners.

We could probably do a feature article on just the interior, but we'll give you the highlights. Steering is initiated via a vintage Mooney yoke (basically a plane's steering wheel). A Hurst shifter that's been modified to accept a Russian MIG joystick stirs the gears. The Peterbilt dash panel has been stuffed with an assortment of vintage gauges, including those made by Stewart-Warner and Keith-Landis. A World War II-era speedometer is connected to a MIG-sourced pilot tube attached to the grille.

CHRIS WALKER'S BUGLY

In 2014, extreme builder Chris Walker reached deep into his mad-scientist mind and pulled out "Bugly." Chris calls it "kind of" a '64 VW because the rear portion of the body is from a humpback '37 Chevy. The two were married together so seamlessly that at first glance it doesn't even look like a custom. It wasn't without effort, though, as Chris says that they cut the quarters of the Chevy "about a dozen times" to get it to look how he wanted it. He tossed the front fenders and customized the hood with a set of Buick portholes. Out back, he reconstructed the Chevy's trunk to open east-west instead of the standard north-south configuration, and he cut out a huge Maltese cross and filled it with expanded metal; it now functions as a third brake light. The "regular" taillights are old drive-in movie speakers.

Chris hand-fabbed the entire front suspension. He did it multiple times, in fact, due to the size and complexity of the motor. The suspension out back is pretty simple: there is none. To keep within budget, he had to make sacrifices, so he's driving the automotive equivalent of a hardtail. He reports that it still rides and drives (right-hand drive, by the way) fairly well, but he runs a lower air pressure in the rear tires to soften things up just a tad. He built

Looking like an angry insect from the front, and with a stylized Maltese cross in back, Bugly offers a smooth ride in addition to its unique appearance.

CHRIS WALKER'S BUGLY

Even More Extreme

There are limits to every automotive scene as well as instances where something is either so far out there, so unique, or so inventive that it can't be classified. There are pseudo-rat rods on the fringe that fall into this group. Some maintain their vintage bodies, but that's all that is "rat rod" about the vehicles. We've seen rat rod tanks, for instance, which are basically vintage cars or trucks with tracks, and even an actual army tank chassis. We've seen all types of way-out-there machines, and if they have any resemblance to rat rods at all, they have probably been referred to as rat rods. Most of these creations are downright cool, fascinating, and extreme works of art, even if they're not technically rat rods.

the frame completely from scratch out of tubing, as opposed to the 2 × 3 he used last year. The tubing offered up its own set of challenges because Chris had never used a tubing bender before.

The centerpiece to the whole build is the 470-cubic-inch 1958 Continental engine that came out of a Cessna airplane. It's an air-cooled flat six that was fuel injected and turbo charged in its flying days. Chris opted to build his own intake manifolds and plop a couple of four-barrels on top. They're both Edelbrocks, but one's a 650 and one's a 600, owing to the fact that they were what he could get from the swap meet.

The car ran, but didn't run well. It wasn't until the team got on tour that they figured out the issue. They ran a balance tube from one intake to the other, which made the engine run smoothly and powerfully. Cruising on the freeway at a leisurely 1800 RPM through the 700R4, there's oodles of torque available anytime. And even with eight barrels of Edelbrock choking down the fuel, Bugly gets 11 MPG on the freeway.

One of the stops on the tour was the set of Stacey David's *GearZ*. This is a guy who's pretty much seen and done it all related to cars and trucks, and even he couldn't get enough of Bugly. In fact, one of the staff members wouldn't let Chris go without a quick spin around the neighborhood. The car even sounds like it should, with that angry wasp's-nest snarl of the big flat six at WOT.

SURVIVORS

Rat rod culture isn't just about mashing things together, throwing big engines into little cars, or building aggressive low-riding Model As. There's a part of rat rod culture that embraces American steel in a more traditional way. Such a vehicle—a survivor—is often close to original. Its outward appearance may be that of a distressed, weather-worn, or even decrepit "junker," but it may have an updated drivetrain. Or it may be an old, dirty vehicle that has been meticulously brought back to life through mechanical resuscitation. Maybe it has a modern engine or added horsepower.

Farm trucks are good examples of survivors and are very common in rat rod culture. On the outside, you see an old-looking original 1940s or '50s pickup, but it is in good running and driving condition. Some vehicles from the '60s or later also fall into this category, even if they're not technically considered rat rods. We often refer to '50s and '60s cars that are in their original state as "derelicts," and they are right on the edge of what we'd call a rat rod and a survivor. It could be one, the other, or maybe both? Or maybe it's just an old car that would be considered a classic if cleaned up.

PHIL LECLARE'S PONTIRAT

A perfect example of a survivor is Phil LeClare's "Pontirat," a 1953 Pontiac Chieftan that Phil has maintained as a daily driver. It's a simple, solid, drivable piece of rolling history with all of the cool aesthetic features you'd see on a rat rod: rust, patina, and plenty of visible wear and tear from ol' Mother Nature.

Phil LeClare drives his Pontiac survivor on a daily basis.

PHIL LECLARE'S PONTIRAT

Dan Larson's 1938 Ford pickup retains the look of its original exterior.

DAN LARSON'S 1938 FORD

Our explanation of survivors wouldn't be complete without at least one rat rod pickup truck. This 1938 Ford owned by Dan Larson runs a 305 Chevy engine but looks like an original pickup on the outside. Of course, Dan added his own personal touches to the truck, but he captured the essence of a 1938 Ford. There are many survivor-esque rat rod pickups similar to this: fairly original with personal touches, some modifications, and new (or newer) mechanical components.

THE MOORES' HANDYMAN WAGON

This beautiful 1955 Chevy Handyman owned by Rick and Casey Moore in Belfry, Montana, is a great example of a fully functional survivor with some nice modifications. It's not entirely original, but it definitely looks original. The wagon's frame has been modified to allow a C4 Corvette suspension to be bolted to it. The suspension and rear axle are all stock Corvette parts, and a hydroboost brake system was added for reliability. Wheels are Budnik billet, and the tires are Goodyear Eagle F-1. Under the hood is an LS-1 motor out of a 2000 C5 Corvette with all of the accessories. Modern guts, classic body.

The Handyman is a 1955 Chevy wagon with its original look and some modern upgrades.

THE MOORES' HANDYMAN WAGON

CHAD TRUSS'S 1955 DODGE

Chad Truss, who contributed most of the photography for this book, has his own rat rod that falls into the survivor category. Photographed by Jared Levine for *Rat Rod Magazine*, Chad's 1955 Dodge looks fairly original. But it's not.

After spending a couple of years as photography director for *Rat Rod*, Chad decided that he was going to challenge himself by building a rat rod of his own. Simple enough, right? He was gravitating toward an early 1930s sedan, but then he got wind of another project. One of his tuner-car buddies had a '55 Dodge pickup that, at one time, was to be a father-son restoration project. As so often happens with these projects, other things came up, and time got away—fifteen years later, the truck was just another piece of lawn art. It turns out that the price was right for Chad. The owner was looking for a new camera, and Chad happened to have one that he was willing to let go of for the nominal price of … one 1955 Dodge pickup.

Rat Rod Magazine photographer Chad Truss traded a camera for the 1955 Dodge truck that he transformed in to a low, lean machine.

It was a pretty solid old truck when he got it, with the odometer showing only about 37,000 miles. It had been used as a farm truck and didn't often stray far from home. Chad soon discovered that the flathead six engine was stuck. Thus, the first order of business was getting it unstuck. After liberally bathing every cylinder with PB Blaster, he was able

CHAD TRUSS'S 1955 DODGE

to turn the motor over by hand. Amazingly, after a carb rebuild and some basic tune-up parts, the engine roared to life! The three-on-the-tree tranny shifted perfectly without so much as checking the lube. Chad added a set of tires and did some other miscellaneous fixing and tweaking, and that's how he drove the truck for the first year.

Many people either would have been satisfied at this point or would have gone the full restoration route. Not Chad. He had bigger plans. He knew that a metamorphosis was about to take place in the name of both drivability and general (bad) attitude. Over a period of about thirty days, the truck was reengineered from front to back and top to bottom. The original frame was discarded and one from a Chevy S-10 was shortened by 6 inches (and fully boxed) to match the Dodge's wheelbase and inserted in place.

Note the low stance of the truck. What's cool about the Dodge is that the body is channeled over the frame from the factory. This meant that Chad could get that low, lean look without extensive body mods and that he could cruise in comfort and style. Chad was very specific about not altering the body. Brakes, steering, and suspension all came from the same S-10 in the name of cost and simplicity. The badass steelies were custom made to Chad's specs by the guys at Pete Paulsen Motorsports.

Once everything was buttoned up, it was time for the shakedown run. And shake it did, as the rear end gave out in the first 100 yards of the test drive. Chad sourced another one, and, within another day, the truck was on the road. But, as so often happens with builds like this, gremlins pop up. The 400 SBC never quite ran right and wound up burning a couple valves. As of this writing, Chad and the crew had just sourced a freshly built 350 and dropped it in, and, at last report, all signs pointed to a full recovery.

RAY "MOUSE" DOLPH'S 1948 FORD

Our friend Ray "Mouse" Dolph from Canada saved this 1948 Ford pickup from its abandonment. Ray had been working on a Chevy Nova project when he came across a 1948 Ford F47 truck body half buried in the mud. The owner of the truck said, "If you can dig it out, you can have it." And that's how it began. Most rat rod projects seem to begin with people coming across free car parts.

Over the course of three days, Ray dug out the pickup. After that, he went to the salvage yard to lok for a suitable donor vehicle to use for a frame and drivetrain, and he found a 1991 Chevy S-10. It was in running order and perfect for the project.

The S-10 frame swap is very common in the world of rat rods. The frame is easy to set a V-8 into, the parts are cheap, and they are about the right size. Most people who use S-10 frames for their rat rods ditch everything else and use just the frame. Ray, however, decided to use the 4.3-L fuel-injected V-6 drivetrain and all for this project.

Ray "Mouse" Dolph finished this 1948 Ford F47 truck build in time for the 2012 Rat Rod Tour.

Ray pulled the body off the S-10 but grafted the cab floor and firewall underneath the Ford cab. This allowed the Ford cab to bolt right up to the frame, and the transmission tunnel was already correct for the drivetrain.

To match the S-10 wheelbase, Ray made a truck bed using 1948 Chevy bed sides and fenders, but he used the Ford end panel and tailgate. The floor of the bed is old barn wood.

Ray built the truck in five months, working in the evenings and on some weekends. He got it running just in time for the 2012 Rat Rod Tour. The drive to Las Vegas and back was this truck's maiden voyage, and Ray made the 4,600-mile trek with zero issues.

RANDY "FARMBOY" LARSON'S 1947 FORD

Everybody has asked for a second chance for some reason or another, but how often does somebody actually get one? Better yet, how many people get a *second* second chance? Ask Randy "Farmboy" Larson about his 1947 Ford pickup, and he'll tell you. This sweet old truck was headed for the crusher when a friend of Randy's swooped in and saved it—only to lose interest and prepare to send it to the crusher himself. But that's when our hero stepped in. Randy was actually looking for a '48–'50 Ford pickup, but when he found out about this one, he snapped it up. It was fairly complete, missing only the drivetrain, wheels, and an axle.

After those two close calls, you'd think that Randy got right to work on this beast, right? Well, not exactly. The car sat in his pole barn for quite a while before Randy commenced with the build. In fact, he went as far as putting the truck up for sale once he had dropped in the engine. *Rat Rod* came across the truck in a Craigslist ad while in search of material for our first Tour Rat, and we almost bought it! But such things happen (or don't happen) for a reason, and Randy wound up completing the truck.

The bodywork on this '47 is courtesy of Henry Ford and Mother Nature. Randy has touched neither a panel nor a fender, and the truck retains all of its stock parts along with the patina of a life spent outdoors in Minnesota. Randy has resisted the common trend to mercilessly slice and dice the body, and thus it retains the same profile (albeit a bit lower) as it did many decades ago. This theme carries over to the interior, where it's pretty much all '47 Ford. This truck may be retirement age, but it's just getting started!

This 1947 Ford pickup had two close calls with the crusher before Randy Larson rescued it.

RANDY "FARMBOY" LARSON'S 1947 FORD

Randy enhanced the truck's already-low profile.

TOP INSET: Exterior "paint" provided by the great outdoors in the form of natural patina that's so desirable in rat rods.

BOTTOM INSET: Modifications for speed and power lie under the original hood.

We mentioned the truck's low profile. No bags here! Randy Z'd the frame by 6 inches front and rear. Up front is an axle from a '62 F100 with a Speedway drop spindle kit, augmented with disc brakes for safety and drivability. A Dana 44 posi out of a 1980 IH Scout II puts the power to the asphalt out back.

And power there is under the hood in the form of a Ford 302 punched-out .040 over. Go-fast goodies include a Weiand tunnel ram supporting a couple of Holley 450s, an Accel coil, and a Pertronix distributor to keep the sparks a-sparkin'. Properly passing the spent gasses was not an easy feat for Randy due to the pesky steering linkage. The passenger side was a snap with a stock Mustang HO tubular header, but the driver's side took several hours of fabrication to rework an Explorer GT-40 header for proper fit. As for a transmission, cogs are swapped by a proper four-speed, donated by an '81 Mustang Cobra.

The 3.07 gears out back plus the overdrive transmission allow Randy to squeeze about 15 MPG out of his rig. That makes things much easier on the wallet with all of the driving he does, especially when his four-year-old daughter, Amber, is always saying, "Daddy, go faster!" and urging Randy to race every car that pulls up next to them.

COLD WAR MOTORS

While on the topic of survivors, Rick Loxton might shed some light from a different perspective on the subject. Rick profiled a Canadian gentleman by the name of Scott Newstead, who, for lack of a better term, saves cars. Not big-dollar collectibles, but clunkers or decrepit lost souls. While Scott is not saving or building rat rods, what he does is something that may inspire those within the rat rod scene to look at things a little differently.

The Internet has been called both the greatest invention ever as well as the work of the devil himself. Somewhere in the middle, you can find some really useful information, like how to rope a calf, walk on hot coals, or cook a complete meal under the hood of your car. Nestled somewhere among kitten videos and Amish dating sites is a place called Cold War Motors (CWM), the spawn of the fertile mind of Alberta, Canada's Scott Newstead.

Scott's blog (coldwarmotors.blogspot.com) takes an unprecedented look "behind the curtain" at an inept, bat-crap crazy, insane bureaucracy of Scott's creation, loosely based on the job that his dad held for several years in the Canadian government. CWM blends his dad's experiences with those of Scott and his friends while they spend their time acquiring as many $500 cars as possible with little or no hope of ever restoring any of them.

"My idea was to have an anti-car blog. There were too many people going, 'Ooooh, look! I welded this panel on my Chevelle.' It's not a 'look-what-I-can-do' blog but more of a jab at me and my friends. We make a point of driving the foulest cars we can. It's kind of the middle finger toward the whole consumer thing. Anything with a three-digit price, and I'm right there!"

Cold War Motors' YouTube channel (www.youtube.com/user/coldwarmotors) is a must-see for anybody who appreciates crusty old cars. Scott is a collector of old cars, but he's not your typical car collector. His idea of fun is to find a car that was parked sometime before he was born (40+ years ago, if you must know) and get it back to running condition with a budget of $0. Add to this that many of the cars are orphan brands that haven't been sold new since Eisenhower was president, and you can see how challenging this can be.

One day, Scott decided to film the process and share it with his friends. They dug it and immediately suggested that he put it on YouTube. Once the subscribers started rolling in, Scott knew that he had something kind of special. He has plenty of material to work with, having a couple dozen derelict cars in his yard that represent many different makes, models, and nationalities.

"I have to move the cars around anyway, so I'll get them running. Their looks don't diminish the integrity of the collection. It's my collection. A lot of it is just keeping them out of the crusher. In the meantime, I'll get them running and drive them around the yard. It's about wrenching with your friends. To relax, I work on my own

One of Scott Newstead's junkyard rescues.

rusty cars and not worry about it. I like walking past them. I like leaning on fenders of old cars with my buds. They come here to get away from whatever they are doing."

Once he gets a car running, that's it. He'll drive it around, park it, and start on the next worthless project. In the meantime, he has given that car one last bit of dignity. Something that was once somebody's pride and joy is able to take at least one last victory lap of sorts. And then it will rest again under the watchful eyes of Scott and his buddies.

CWM's YouTube channel also offers plenty of great junkyard tours. Again, Scott's always cruising junkyards anyway, so why not film it and share it with the world? It's a real treat because Scott has access to some of the coolest junkyards you could ever imagine. No Camrys or Cavaliers here—just lots of pre-1970 iron! Because a lot of these cars are going to be crushed, Scott figures that it's a great idea to document and preserve their images before they disappear.

There is too much more to mention here, but suffice it to say that there is a little something for every car lover out there. Restorations, test drives, hoonage, and more. What can we look forward to from Scott? "There's no shortage of stupid decisions to write about. I'll be buying three rusty Saab 99s with no time to restore them." Yep— just another day at Cold War Motors.

WHAT A RAT ROD IS NOT

There is definitely such a thing as "too new" to be a rat rod. As much as some people like to call their modern vehicles rat rods—either because they are rusty, made of mismatched parts, or whatever other reason—there is no such thing as a modern rat rod. The whole soul of rat rodding is tied into hot rod culture. Being a hot rod counterculture, rat rodding has to live somewhere within those limits as well. A modern car with rat rod styling is more of a custom or modified than it is a rat rod. Same with any other additions to a modern car. As written previously in this book and in multiple *Rat Rod Magazine* articles, there is a limit to what is and what is not a rat rod. A 1995 Toyota with a rusty hood and a chop top is simply a modified 1995 Toyota.

Sometimes art cars are also labeled as rat rods. It's not uncommon for rat rods to have themes, multiple ornaments, relics, or other "artful" features, but a car that is overwhelmingly decorated should fall into the art-car category, especially if it is lacking that vintage body. If it's built purely for its "shock factor," it's hard to classify it as a rat rod.

Just because we don't label a car as a rat rod doesn't mean that it isn't cool. It's just not a rat rod. Art cars? They can be very cool and awesomely creative. Same with any kind of modified vehicle, custom, classic—they all have their own charms and die-hard enthusiasts, and, hey, someone put their passion into them, which is always a point of respect.

Rat rod culture is very tolerant, which is one of the things that many of its detractors are not. Respect is sacred within the rat rod community and earned by those who put passion into their vehicles, no matter what it is. Many people applaud rat rodders for their positive and accepting nature. The Rat Rod Tour, for example, is known for its comradery, "family" vibe, and drama-free atmosphere, values that reflect the core of rat rodding.

Because of the blue-collar, necessity-driven foundation on which the rat rod scene is built, there is far less ego and pageantry than in other parts of automotive world. That's not to say that there is no pride—because there is. There is also confidence, and oftentimes competition, but it is friendlier, almost like good ol' buddies trying to one-up each other. In the end, it's all about fellowship and the bonds created through the builds and the drives.

9
Common Parts

FARM TRUCKS

Old farm trucks are a huge part of rat rod culture, mostly because of their distressed, worn-out appearance. Many of these pickups are left in their original condition on the outside but equipped with new drivetrains and mechanical components on the inside.

ENGINES

Rat rods are known for being unpainted and having a lot of rust, distress, and other imperfections, but one thing that has no limits is the size, style, make, or cost of the engine. Many rat rods have rebuilt or even old, used engines; some are found at the scrap yard, freshened up, and brought back to life. Some are brand-new crate engines; some are powerful full-blown horsepower monsters. There is no right and wrong when it comes to the power plant. The rat rod scene sees a lot of vintage motors, like old flatheads, revered for their aesthetic quality, as well as rare and peculiar motors, such as old V-12s, diesel engines of all shapes and sizes, and other oddities from the past. Hemi,

ENGINES

Modified Ford flathead.

A trio of carbs.

A rare early Buick 264 nailhead.

A ubiquitous small-block Chevy.

A small-block Ford with a high-rise manifold.

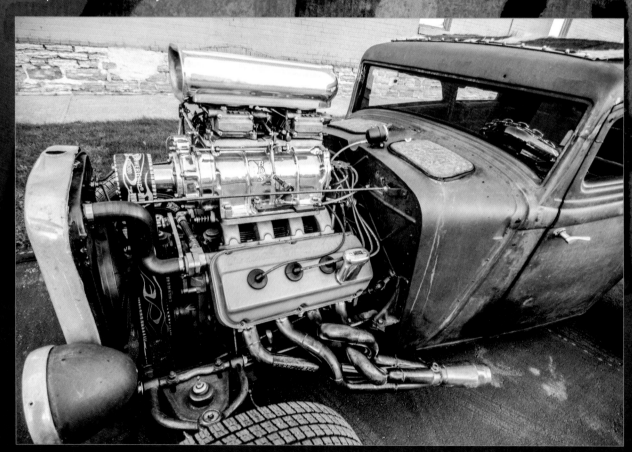

An early Chrysler Hemi.

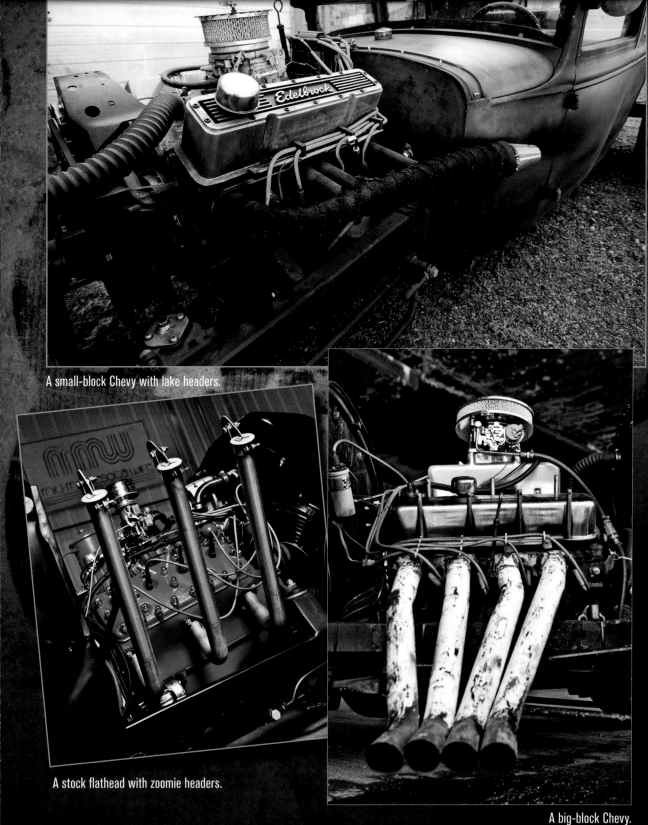

A small-block Chevy with lake headers.

A stock flathead with zoomie headers.

A big-block Chevy.

Olds Rocket valve covers on a small-block Chevy.

Cummins Diesel, Olds big block, Cadillac—there are so many different options, and rat rodders will use them all. Can you identify all nine of the engines pictured?

Progress drastically altered the power-plant landscape of the traditional-style rat rod. The go-to engine back in the day was either the Ford 4-cylinder or the ubiquitous Ford flathead V-8. Immensely popular even in their stock forms, enterprising companies leveraged this popularity into what we now call the "aftermarket," making it simple and relatively inexpensive to realize measurable gains in horsepower and torque.

In a cataclysmic shift that is still felt to this day, General Motors introduced the much more powerful overhead valve V-8 in 1949 in both the Cadillac and Oldsmobile brands. These new engines could breathe much easier because they were more efficient at moving fuel and air in and out of the combustion chamber. The move was a game-changer, and within less than a decade, every major domestic brand had its own V-8 engine. But it was Chevrolet's version, which debuted in 1955, that has become the engine of choice for rat rodders, hot rodders, drag racers—you name it. The small-block Chevy, and more specifically the 350-cubic-inch version, is popular for its perfect combination of availability, flexibility, and adaptability.

Sometimes old valve covers are used to add a vintage look to newer engines. Keeping an engine, or the vehicle in general, "old school" on the outside is extremely important in the rat rod scene.

INTERIORS

Rat rod interiors are often left unfinished, much like their bodies. That's not to say that builders don't put care into their interiors. Many rat rodders use this space to add personal touches and to repurpose items that have sentimental or historical significance. Many creature comforts are overlooked, leaving a stripped-down, functional interior.

One of the more creative touches inside a rat rod is often the shifter knob or the entire shifter itself. It's not uncommon to see high shifters and knobs made from all manner of weaponry, skulls, sculptures, or custom-made metal objects.

An almost stock rat rod interior without the usual personalization.

The shifter is typically the focal point of the interior, and thus is often a reflection of the builder's personality.

PERSONAL TOUCHES

You'll see a variety of vintage relics displayed on and in rat rods, many with historic significance. Badges, plates, tags, and other antiques are extremely popular. Hood ornaments are another way to personalize vehicles, and, as with many automotive components, there are a lot to choose from. Rat rodders often enjoy the thrill of searching for, discovering, and selecting old, rare, or odd pieces.

Old license plates are very common, especially since you can actually register them in many states (in others, you cannot, or the process is long and complicated). Rat rodders also often collect license plates to hang inside their cars as decorations or to patch holes.

Rat rods have developed this sort of aggressive Mad-Max quality that is sometimes accentuated by spikes, riveted steel, and other industrial post-apocalyptic elements.

Rat rodders often use odd or sometimes rare objects as hood ornaments.

Over the years, rat rodders have embraced some of the showmanship and entertainment elements of the scene, to the delight of spectators and enthusiasts. As such, a popular addition to a rat rod is any variety of flame thrower. Most rat rodders use a simple system of igniting gas fumes by using a spark plug, which sends flames out of an exhaust pipe.

We can't overlook the tractor– automobile connection, either. While it has become less common in recent years, many rat rodders have used tractor grilles or other farm- implement parts in their rat rods. It ties the rat rod scene back to its doodlebug roots.

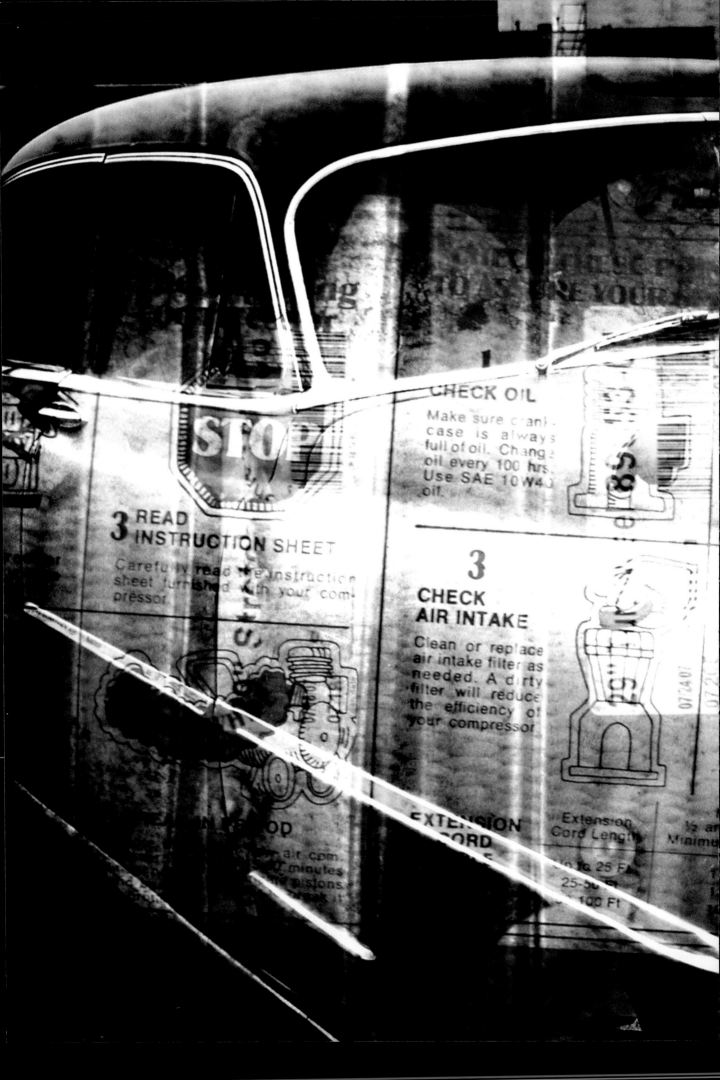

10
Building Practices

It can't be stressed enough how important safety is when you're building a rat rod or any kind of modified vehicle. Rat rods are usually devoid of any safety systems such as anti-lock brakes, air bags, or traction control, so it's paramount to take care at every phase of the build to ensure the safety of the driver, the passengers, and fellow motorists.

istorically, rat rods have been derided for not only their lack of paint but also for a perceived lack of both quality construction and safety. Of course, these opinions and views are often formed based on appearances. Rust and mismatched parts can give the impression that the vehicle is unsafe, but most rat rods hide mechanically sound and structurally safe machines behind their worn-out exteriors.

Although rat rods are generally built to be durable, safe, and ultimately functional, there is always going to be a fringe element in every genre that gives the rest of the group a bad name, and it would be disingenuous not to acknowledge it. Some have misinterpreted the inherent rebel element of the rat rod culture and used it as a license to employ cracked and weathered tires, eliminate floorboards, and use substandard welding, all in the name of being the "bad boy" of the scene. These practices are misguided at best and life-threatening at worst.

Compared to the modern marvels of safety that are built today, every facet of the hot rod hobby, including rat rodding, is burdened with the issue of safety in general. Take a look at a fiberglass T-bucket, with its steamroller tires in the rear, bicycle wheels up front, and some kind of outrageous (usually supercharged) V-8 in the middle. How about a 1960s muscle car? In some cases, you had a 300- to 400-horsepower car with four-wheel drum brakes and a 20:1 steering ratio.

Perhaps the best way to demonstrate a healthy build is to share some of *Rat Rod Magazine*'s documented builds. One of the most popular builds in *Rat Rod* history is the $1,500 blue-collar build and instructional guide by Tommy Ring. This is a man who understands not only the very essence of rat rod culture but also how to communicate to people who want to get out and try to build. His instructional series have captivated *Rat Rod* readers, and no rat rod historical compendium would be complete without his insight and direction. So, in this chapter, we present an adaptation of Tommy Ring's step-by-step $1,500 rat rod build guide along with documentation from the 2011, 2012, 2013, and 2015 *Rat Rod* Tour Rat builds.

NSRA

The National Street Rod Association (NSRA) offers a free 23-point inspection at their events with the main goal of calling "the owner's attention to something which may have been overlooked ... an extra set of eyes to notice a potentially life-threatening condition before it becomes more of one."

TOMMY RING'S $1500
RAT ROD BUILD

THE BODY

Finding a cheap and workable, yet cool, body starts with a little imagination. Points to ponder: if you choose a car from the '50s or '60s, you need to consider the pros and cons. If you buy a 1950 Hudson, for instance, where will you get a door or a hood if you need one? Remember that crap happens, and unless there is a Hudson junkyard in your area, you may want to pass. Just sayin'! The truth is, when you spot that dream car, ego kicks in and sense flies out the window. Remember, we are talking low budget. Rat rods are defined by many enthusiasts as cars from 1963 and earlier, and any of those years will work—just be sure that all parts are intact unless you know where to find cheap spare parts for that model. The 1920s and 1930s are my personal favorites because it is easy to fabricate patch panels for them—with some 22-gauge steel, a cutting tool, and a welder, you can work wonders. They also look pretty cool no matter how you build them, although they are pretty pricey!

BODY

To keep with our low-budget theme, I suggest a pickup for a few reasons. First, it doesn't have to be a 1932 Ford truck to look cool—any of the trucks from the 1950s and earlier will work, and, best of all, they're cheap. At most swap meets, I've noticed that cabs such as old Fords, Chevys, Internationals, and others in the late '40s and early to mid-'50s start out in the morning at around $850. By mid-afternoon, they're marked down to $700, and by closing time, they're down to $500. On three occasions, I've offered $300 for a pickup just as they were packing up to haul home, and I wound up the proud owner each time. The great thing about these old trucks is that there are so many options on how to build them. You can run fenders or not, you can chop and channel them for that open-wheel low-rider look, or you can channel, section, and cut the top off and go for a roadster look.

These old rusty $300–$500 cabs will require some sweat equity, but that's part of the fun. If the doors and latches are rusted shut, a shot of PB Blaster every day for two to three weeks will cure the problem. If the hinges are gone, they're pretty easy to make with a piece of flat stock and small piece of pipe, and you can rob the pins from old barn hinges. Glass is not an issue, because flat glass for the sides and back is cheap. A windshield can be glued in if necessary. If the title isn't available, swap-meet titles for the late '40s and '50s usually cost around $50 as opposed to a 1930 Model A title at $500–$800. See, we are saving money already!

Now that we have a cab, where do we start? If it has a seat, take it out and weld ½-inch rebar from the left front corner to the right rear corner and from the right front corner to the left rear corner. Also, tack-weld the doors in place in three small spots. This will keep the cab square and the doors in place when we begin cutting the cab up.

The floor needs to go, so mark up 6 inches or whatever you prefer with a marker about every 2 feet to stay consistent. Connect the lines with a level and get out your Sawzall or circular saw with an abrasive blade and cut the line all the way around. Lift the cab off the old floor and set it on a good level spot on the ground. We will mark up 4 inches in the front and in the back where the frame will sit, so the cab will hide the frame and sit a little lower as well.

Now is the time to decide which style of rod you want to build. For our example, we will build one open-wheel, open-motor, low-rider type and one roadster type.

THE FRAME

I realize that you could get a Chevy S-10 frame and be done, and if you were running fenders, that would be fine. However, if you want that open-wheeled roadster look, all of that front suspension can look gaudy. For less money and a cooler look, I would suggest building a frame. Don't panic! It's not as complicated as it sounds, and we will walk you through it step by step.

The recipe starts with two 12-foot sticks of 2 × 3 × ⅛-inch wall-thickness rectangular tubing and one 8-foot stick. Some general measurements to keep in mind: Ford, Chevy, and Dodge cabs measure 57 inches from the back of the cab to the front of the bottom firewall. V-8 motors require 36 inches from the bell housing to the radiator. Most truck rod beds are from 36 to 48 inches long, and the frame measures 26½ inches wide in the front, inside to inside, and 32 inches wide in the back, inside to inside. Allowing for the tubing to be 2 inches wide will give you 30½ inches outside to outside in the front and 36 inches outside to outside in the back.

Your first cut will be the front inside tube, which is cut to 26½ inches but with a 5-degree cut on both sides to allow for the frame to flare wider as it goes back. Next, cut two 36-inch pieces for the section that the motor sits on, two 15-inch pieces for the L kick-ups in the back, and three 32-inch pieces for pick-up bed rails and an inside piece to connect them. Finally, cut two pieces 63 inches from a square cut on one end to the long point of a 45-degree cut.

Mark a straight chalk line on the floor with a square and place the two 36-inch pieces with the 26½-inch piece between them. You can check it with your square, but remember that it is not 90 degrees because your frame widens as it goes back. It helps to lay your frame pieces out end-to-end, allowing for 26½ inches in the front and 32 inches inside at the back; this will give you an idea of what the frame flare will look like.

Tack the first three pieces together for the front section. Next, take the two 15-inch pieces and tack them to the blunt ends of the 63-inch pieces to give you the L kick-up for the back. Then measure 58 inches from the inside of the Ls on both sides, and this will be where your cab will sit. Place the front section on top of the 63-inch pieces and tack it in place on the 58-inch lines. This 3-inch Z will give you extra clearance for your oil pan in the front, and the overlap of about 6 inches will give you a long welding surface to attach the front to the middle section.

Next, take the three 32-inch pieces and tack them together with one in between the other two; this will give you a 36-inch width for your bed section. This section needs to be set up on top of the 15-inch Ls with a bucket holding it up in back until you can level it out and then tack the back section to the two Ls.

At this point, pull a tape measure from the front corner to the opposite rear corner and vice versa. This will tell you if your frame is square and if the measurement is the same; if not, tweak it until it is.

This part of the build will take about an hour and a half of your time and $100 in steel costs. If you can't weld, you can hire a welder in his off time—it will still be much cheaper overall than buying a frame, and it will look much cooler.

REAR END

We could've chosen a late '80s to mid-'90s Crown Vic or Merc rear end, and all of the brackets would have already been there. Instead, we chose a plain-Jane Dodge unit with no brackets to demonstrate how to set it up. First, you determine ride height and set your frame on blocks. We set ours on 2 × 8s that are 7¼ inches. Remember, your rod will settle a good 2 inches after the drivetrain and all accessories are on board.

Next, roll your rear end under the frame and measure from the front on both sides to a stationary point on the rear end. Measure from the backing plate to the frame as well. Once it's measured out and you know that it's straight and centered, tack a piece of rebar from the rear end up to the frame. This will hold it in place until all of the brackets are welded on and completed. Also scotch the tires in place with blocks so it won't roll out of square.

Find a pair of rear coil springs from a small car; they are cheap and easy to jig up. Get a piece of pipe that will fit snug into the coils and cut it into 4-inch pieces. Slide one into the bottom of each coil and set it on your rear end about 1½ inches away from the frame and inside. Level it so it's straight and then tack the pipe to the top of the rear end (no solid welds until we're completely jigged up). The coil should be free to slide on and off the pipe. Next, weld a 4 × 4½-inch steel plate to the 4-inch pipes and drill a ½-inch hole in the center. This will mount down into the tops of the coils to hold them steady and straight.

You can weld a 6 × 6½-inch steel plate to each side of the frame to hold your coil tops, or you can use L brackets (like we have for taller coils). The more you cut off your coils, the stiffer your ride will be. Use ½-inch bolts to secure your coils to the frame. You will need two 2 × 3-inch straps of ½-inch steel for your traction bars. Line them up in a straight line to your frame. Tack them to the bottom of the rear end, spaced out to accommodate a piece of 2 × 2-inch square tube (or whatever you choose to use as traction bars). The front of the traction bars will need ½-inch steel straps welded to them to straddle the frame. You will need to drill ½-inch holes in these straps to belt through the frame on the front and between the straps of the bottom of the rear end. This allows the rear end to move up and down freely. Next, you will tack two 2 × 6-inch ½-inch steel straps to the far side of the center section of the rear end for your anti-sway bar. You will need two more steel straps of the same size to mount inside the frame. A piece of ¾-inch pipe with heim joints mounted will serve as your bar. The heim

joints will allow the rear end to move up and down but will stop all side-to-side movement; you can also use ball joints to accomplish the same thing.

Next, you will need a bar from the front center of your rear end to a stationary plate or tube running across the frame tops, where the cab will sit. This bar prevents the rear end from pitching up every time you stomp on the gas pedal. This bar also needs two ½-inch straps to mount to— on both the rear end and the frame cross-member. It can be set up with heim joints on each end for adjustment purposes and to allow up-and-down movement.

Last, you will need ½-inch brackets welded onto the rear end for shock mounts. They can be on the front or the rear of the rear end. We put them on the rear to allow more room up front for the gas tank and battery. Half-inch steel straps will serve as bottom mounts off the rear end, and you can attach the top to the 6 × 6-inch plates holding the coil springs or to a bar added across the frame.

There are several ways to set up a rear end, but this way is probably the least expensive if you can't find one already set up with all of the brackets. Remember to remove the rebar that you tacked in to steady the rear end while you were setting it up.

FRONT END

Of all of the things you can do to your rod, nothing will be as important as the front suspension. If you're running fenders, there are several options. On the other hand, without fenders, the choices are slim if you want your rod to look like the real McCoy. In our case, we're talking about a cheap hot rod, so this narrows it down even more. You need an inexpensive option to keep your rod looking cool while being safe, which is a must. The hot ticket starts with a straight axle off any truck, no matter the year or make. The beauty of this setup is that your kingpins, hubs, brakes, and so forth are already there, saving you a ton. This type of axle typically costs between $50 and $100 (unless it has new brakes and wheel cylinders). Don't pay more.

The first step is to get rid of the leaf springs. At this point, your rear end is completed with the frame still on blocks. Roll your front axle up to the front of the frame and measure a center line on the axle and one on the frame. Match the two and measure from the back wheels to the front to make sure that the axle is centered and running straight.

The next step is to install a part on which we have patent-pending status. It is available through my website, *www.ringrods.com*, and will allow you to do a traverse spring setup on any straight axle. You bolt or weld the part to the two pads on your axle where the leaf springs were attached, and it becomes the key to your front-end setup. The top hole is for your shock mount, which will also serve as your headlight mounting bracket. The center hole will be for your spring perch (available at any speed shop), and the top and bottom holes are for your hairpin radius rods (discussed a few paragraphs later).

With spring perches bolted on, you will need shackles (available at any Tractor Supply) to mount a 28- to 30-inch leaf spring (also available at any Tractor Supply or trailer-supply house) to the spring perches on either side of axle. You will need to weld a center bracket to the front of the frame so that you can bolt a standard leaf-spring attachment kit to it. With traverse spring mounts, you will see where to locate the center weld bracket, because different axles will sit at different heights.

Before locking all of this down, put a degree finder on your axle or kingpins and pitch your axle backward 6–10 degrees. This is called "positive caster" and is very important for several reasons: it puts the weight of the rod at the back of the wheels, which makes for easier steering, and it helps pull your wheels back straight after coming out of a curve. It also helps with front-end wandering and prevents rollover when you hit the brakes hard. The axle will have a tendency to roll forward in a hard stop.

The next step is the previously mentioned hairpin radius rods. You can make them from ¾-inch pipe with a nut welded to one end, a clevis yoke screwed through the nut, and a jam nut for adjustment. Two pipes with this setup will narrow to a 3-inch section of ¾-inch pipe between them with a nut welded to it, a heim joint screwed through it, and a jam nut for adjustment.

These radius rods will differ in length according to your rat rod's setup but are usually around 30 inches long. The two clevis yokes on the front of the radius rods will bolt through upper and lower holes on your mounting bracket, and the rear heim joint will bolt through a 2-inch strap of ½-inch-thick steel that is welded to the side of your frame. A 10-foot piece of ¾-inch pipe should cost approximately $12, and the four clevis yokes and two heim joints should cost less than $50, making your total cost for a set of radius rods around (or even a little less than) $60.

The next step is two pieces of steel, 10–12 inches tall, welded to the left and right front frame corners. These pieces will mount your shocks, which will run from the top hole of

Preventing Bump-Steer

A rod mounted with heim joints from frame to axle can also work to prevent bump-steer. The end mounted to the frame should be on the same side as the steering box, diagonal to the opposite side of your axle. This is called a "pan hard bar." Another thing that will help prevent bump-steer is a steering damper mounted from the tie rod to the frame. This part sells for around $40 and will be well worth it.

your mounting bracket to these two pieces. These two pieces will also serve as your headlight-mounting brackets. If you set up your frame as we discussed previously, the distance between the two shock mount pieces will be perfect to mount a 1920s or '30s radiator shell with the headlights setting tight to the shell.

The next step is your steering arm. If you run your axle with the tie rod at the back, there will already be a steering arm attached to the left spindle. If you run the tie rod in front, which is called a suicide setup, you will cut the steering arm off, which will now be on the right side, and make a new steering arm that will attach to the two left top bolts on the spindle. You can make the steering arm from a ⅜-inch to ⁷⁄₁₆-inch angle iron cut down on one side to straddle the kingpin and with holes drilled in it to mount to the spindle; the other side should taper from the width of the spindle holes to about 2½ inches in front.

A hole drilled in the narrowed end of the steering arm can mount a heim joint attached to a ¾-inch pipe, which will become your drag link to the steering box. Most steering boxes will work. If the pitman arm swings in the wrong direction, you can mount it upside down. It may make your pitman arm a top swing or a bottom swing, but the only solution here is to try to keep your drag link as level as possible to prevent bump-steer. Bump-steer is a shaking of the two front wheels that feels like your front end is coming apart, and you definitely don't want that!

One final note: when your front-end setup has the tie rod in front, the Ackermann angle changes. You won't notice it when driving down the road or even in curves, but when maneuvering in parking lots or other tight spaces, you will notice that one tire scoots (or "pushes," as it is called) more than turns. The reason is that your inside tire travels a shorter arc than the outside tire, normally about 3 degrees less. When you reverse your axle, it throws these mathematics off, and there is no correcting it. It's not a big issue because most rods are cruising at slower speeds and not going into curves at high speeds; however, it's worth mentioning.

SETTING THE BODY

Once you have completed setting up the rear end, front-axle system, and rolling chassis, it's time to set the body on the frame. However, let's first stop for a minute and think this over. You could just set your late '40s through late '50s cab on your cool-looking newly formed hand-built frame and be done. But, let me pose a question. This is going to be the rod that you're known for; your own personal statement, right? What if I told you that with just two extra days, you can really make a statement that will set you apart from the crowd?

Think of it this way: you're at a hot rod show, walking down a row of open-wheeled, open-motor truck rods, and sitting next to a really cool '32 Ford truck is a full-size, mid- to late-'50s cab on the same type of frame and setup. The full-size cab really looks funky by comparison. The body dwarfs the motor, no matter how big the motor is (and the height doesn't help). Some chop the tops, and yet it looks like a wide load coming down the road. To change this, take 12 inches out of the center and 6 inches out of the top along with 6 inches off the bottom. The sound of this process freaks out the novice, but I swear it's not a big deal; in fact, let's tackle this project with a '49 Chevy truck, and you'll see that it's not really a big deal after all. The end result is a cab similar in size to the aforementioned '32 Ford and well worth the trouble.

To start, get out your tape measure, 4-foot level, framing square, and magic marker. Set your cab on a level surface and mark up 6 inches all the way around. Cut only after the cab has been secured with X bracing from corner to corner to keep the cab square. In this case, keep one X on one side and one X on the other side because we will be cutting down the middle of the truck.

Find the center of the cab in several places and make a mark on each of them. The front will be easier because you can use the cowl vent, the windshield, or even marks on the firewall to find the center. The rear is a little more difficult, so it may be easier to use your back window to achieve this. Once all of your center marks are made, connect the lines with a 4-foot level from top to bottom, back and front. Now measure over 6 inches on either side of your centerline and make marked lines as well. Remove the glass and then take a reciprocating saw or cutting wheel and cut the 12 inches (or however much you want) out of the center of your truck. If this is your first time attempting this, it will be the hardest thing you've ever done ... but now is not the time to lose courage. I promise that this will work.

Now, with the two truck halves sitting there, it's time to put the puzzle back together. When you bring the two halves together, the first thing you're going to notice is that they don't line up. This is because the later models have a strong contour to the body. Don't panic!

Get out your come-along or body strap and wrap it around the cab. Don't tighten it yet because you have to work it front to back a little at a time. You'll find a spot on the top of your cowl on the edge just in front of the cowl vent. Tack it together. Down a little lower on the firewall, pull it together and tack it in another spot. Now tack together a spot just below the windshield opening.

On a Chevy, there is a widow's peak, and you will find that the peak is still there even after cutting 12 inches out of the middle. Tack your peak together, and it will line up perfectly. The only problem will be that the back half of your cab is at least 16 inches apart. Still no reason to sweat—that is what your strap is for. Just start easing your cab together with the strap or come-along a little at a time. Don't try to do this all in one move. Tack a spot and pull a little.

You will find that on a Ford or Dodge, this process is much easier because the lines are straighter and thus easier to work with. We chose a Chevy because it won't get any harder than that, and yet it will be much easier than you thought. Keep your heat down and your tacks spaced to avoid warping.

Once you've made a little progress tacking and pulling with your strap, keep an eye on your back window opening to make sure that it stays lined up. About now, you will be feeling really fantastic as you see how the body has lined up as if it had been made that way. But joy turns to tears as you look in and see the bottom half of your dash spread open about 4 inches. Again, this is not a big deal. Get on the inside of the truck (you will have to crawl through a window because your doors should still be tacked shut). Take a come-along and hook it onto both door panels and pull them together. You'll find that your dash will come back together perfectly. Your truck will look so cool with 12 inches cut out of it, and you may be tempted to stop there, but don't! We are committed, remember?

Let's get back to the tape measure, level, and square. Find the centerline of the window and windshield openings of your truck, make a series of marks, and connect them with your level. We took 6 inches, so we went 3 inches off the centerline in both directions and continued our cut lines all around the cab. You can true your 6-inch section to be cut out with tape (or freehand if you're steady-handed). It's easier to cut your top line first, set the top out of the way, and then cut the bottom line.

Now that the 6 inches are out of your top, it's time for another decision. You can cut your top into four pieces, line each of them up, and tack strips in between all of the gaps. It will line up with some temporary bracing, and

The Illustrated History of the Rat Rod

all of those body gaps can be filled in. We chose another route: we left the top complete and set it back on as is.

Now here is the trick: in doing this, you will choose whether your back window opening will line up or your side glasses line up. However, two vertical cuts, about 8 inches long, up the back of the cab on each side will settle this issue, and you will find that both the back window opening and the side glass openings will all line up.

Tack up everything temporarily while you deal with the front. Your front post will be a mile from meeting. This is where a torch is a must. Pie-cut notches in the base of your two A pillars and heat them until they meet the top pillars. A flat plate and a C clamp will help make this easier, as will having someone to help you—but I have done it alone, and you can, too.

You may find a slight dip as the two pillars come together. If this is the case, pie-cut three short cuts right above the top of the pillar on the roofline, and this will cure the problem. I realize that there are many ways to chop a top, but we chose this way because we want a laid-back windshield for a more sinister look.

Now is the time to go back and start filling in all of those tacked gaps a little at a time, making sure not to create too much heat. All of the seams can be completely welded shut and ground down to your liking. The one thing left to complete will be your side glass tops. It may take a little pie-cutting on these as well to get them to line up, but it is not too difficult.

Before removing any X bracing or door tacks, go ahead and set your body on the frame. This can be a one-man show with a rope tied through the side windows, hooked on top, and attached to a come-along. This is where your custom-made frame will pay off. If you remember, we measured from the back of the cab to the front of the firewall. That measurement hasn't changed, even with all of the cutting. Your body will sit down in this cradle we created with the frame like it was made for it—because it was made for it. I told you that a homemade frame was the way to go!

The only thing left with our body mount is a lot of leveling. The two notches in the back of the cab discussed previously will allow the cab to sit down over the frame, and you can weld L brackets to the firewall and onto the frame after leveling. Also check to see if it is level from side to side and then weld ¼-inch straps across the frame and attach them in front of and behind the doors. It will now be secure enough for you to move on to the next steps. The floors, made of 18- to 20-gauge and mounted to the straps, will also help steady the body.

One last step on the cab is to make some C straps and mount them across your door bottoms where you cut off the doors. Otherwise, your doors will rattle when you go down the road because you cut 6 inches, including the supports, off your doors. The tacked-in C brackets will make your doors as solid as they ever were.

Now comes the bed, and that will wrap up the body section. Start with 18- to 20-gauge, 20 inches wide and 4 feet long. The best size for a pickup bed, like everything else, is a matter of opinion, but a simple place to start is a box tacked up 4 feet wide and 40 inches long. The two side panels look cooler if you bend a 45-degree angle 4 inches long at the top and weld a ½-inch pipe to the top to give it that old 1950s-style pickup-bed look. You can use ½-inch gas pipe that you can find at Home Depot for around $10 for a 10-foot stick. It welds well and looks finished.

The back and front panels are straight, 20 inches wide by 48 inches long. They make a super-looking pickup bed and should cost less than $40 total. Center the bed and tack it on to the frame with L brackets. Remember to cut slots for the rear-end's up-and-down movement in the side panels at the bottoms. I know all of this creates a few more headaches, but man are you gonna look cool next to the dudes who took short cuts.

STEERING

Now we will tackle setting up a steering box and all of its components. To start, let me dispel some myths. Vega and Corvair boxes are not the only boxes around—just like Ford 9-inch aren't the only rear ends around. We have grown up hearing the same parts, the same lingo, and the same "in" things until we're programmed to think that there are no other options. Thank God that rat rodding has opened the door to a whole new way of thinking. Imaginations are out there, running wild!

There are no limits except the ones you impose, and this is certainly true with steering boxes and setups. You can run Mustang II front ends, rack and pinions, S-10 frames, 1500 round straight axles, or the old truck straight axles (standard 1920s through late '50s) that we've been talking about.

If you think about it, all the box does is turn a pitman arm. If that pitman arm is pointing down when you turn your wheel to the left, the arm will be rotating toward the front of the vehicle. Turning the wheel to the right will bring the pitman arm to the rear of the vehicle. So what if you spot a box and turn the shaft as mentioned and the opposite

effect happens? Simply "180" your pitman arm to work off to the top or flip your box upside down to correct this problem.

But how can you possibly turn a box upside down, considering that your filler cap will then be on the bottom? In all of the years you've had a vehicle, how many times do you remember taking that threaded cap off and adding steering-box grease or oil? Exactly—never. Point being, if you need to add grease, then you've got a bad seal, and it's time for a rebuild or new box.

The next question is: doesn't it hurt the box to run it upside down? Same answer. Only if you're losing oil, which you shouldn't be unless there are seal problems. With this one simple problem out of the way, it opens the door to unlimited possibilities.

The time you're spending trampling through muddy junkyards, looking for that perfect box, can come to a halt. Instead, spend that time looking at the mounting bracket and how you can make that work.

Even a box with the pitman arm underneath and at a slight angle can be turned on its side, and the pitman arm can be heated and straightened, reversed, or changed altogether with another pitman arm. You can match splines just as you can match gears. So, for the purpose of rat rods, which would be the best steering box to use? The answer, of course, is one that is cheap and is not worn out.

You can tell whether a steering box is worn out by taking a pair of vise grips and turning the shaft. Having hard spots in it when you turn it, having a lot of play, or turning harder to the left or right are some of the clues. Also, if it's from a 1958 truck as opposed to a 2008 truck, it's probably going to be more worn. This is not always the case, though; I've bought 1930 boxes that worked perfectly. You just need to check it out before you buy it.

The next points to consider are where and how to mount your steering box. This is only limited by your imagination. You can mount it close to the top of your cowl, with a shaft through the side of the cowl and the pitman arm high, or you can mount it between your brake and gas pedal on the floor,

Note

As a side note, some boxes have a screw on the side that can be adjusted to take some of the play out of the box. There are also rebuild kits available for some boxes, early Ford and Chevy in particular.

By the way, there are steering boxes with long encased shafts, such as International Scout boxes and several other types. If you can't find one of these, you can cut the box shaft before the spline and weld a rod to extend it. Make sure to use a heavy rod, V-groove it, and weld a couple of deep heavy passes on it.

with the shaft through the side of the cowl. With the latter style, you can cut a half-circle at the bottom of the cowl for your pitman arm to swing, and you can close in the top and back for a different look.

Another mounting option is to mount it right outside the firewall. This gives your pitman arm plenty of clearance to attach to your drag link and onto your steering arm. The question becomes how to mount it. Your box style and the swing direction of your pitman arm will determine a lot of this, but a few simple suggestions follow.

You can mount your box on an angled piece welded to the frame, which will be determined by where you want your steering shaft. Some like it higher, and some like it lower. You can temporarily tack a piece of ½-inch to the frame and play with the location of your steering wheel until you get it where you want it, at which point you can weld a heim joint to your dash for your shaft to go through and finish your bracket on the frame, to which you bolt your box.

A great choice for a steering box is a Chevelle box, but it needs to be mounted under, instead of on top of, a bracket. The bracket welds to the outer side of the frame, turns an L, and hangs bolted under the L, turned in toward the motor.

The main key to all of this is to *tack only* until you are sure of your location. There's nothing more uncomfortable than driving a rod with the steering wheel too low or too high. Other steering boxes, like those from '48 to '54 Chevy trucks, will bolt directly into the side of the frame, which makes for a simple setup. These particular boxes have the pitman arm always pointing down and usually hang too low for a low-riding rod, so you may need to shorten the pitman arm and weld it back together.

Any of the '50s to '60s truck boxes work well if they're not too worn. This style of steering is a box with the pitman arm on the left side; the pitman arm will be pointed either down or up, depending on the direction of swing. You will attach a heim joint or tie rod joint—your choice—to the box, and that screws through an adjusting nut, which will be welded into the end of a ¾-inch piece of pipe. The opposite end will have the same setup and be mounted into a steering arm into the top two holes of the spindle mounts.

I suggest making the steering arm from a piece of ⅜- to ½-inch, 6- to 8-inch angle iron. Cut the angle iron to about 5 inches wide, with one side of the angle cut down to around 3 inches and a half circle cut in to straddle your kingpin. Drill two holes to fasten to the top two spindle bracket bolts. The 6- to 8-inch side can be tapered from 5 inches down to 2 inches on the outer side with a ⁷⁄₁₆-inch hole drilled through it. That hole will mount either a heim joint or the tie rod end.

This is the simplest way to go because it involves only your box, pitman arm, drag link, and steering arm. Others prefer a cross-steer setup, which means moving your steering box down closer to the front of the frame. On these setups, the pitman arm will come off the bottom of the box and attach to a rod going to the right side. This arm attaches to an extended tie rod end, and the vehicle steers from the right. Some prefer this setup because the vehicle handles better, with less bump-steer. Having said that, there are some disadvantages. You are more limited with the type of steering box you can use, and the setup requires some knuckle joints. You typically need one knuckle outside of the firewall, attached to a rod going to the steering box, which needs another knuckle to get the rod to drop to the box. In some cases, you need yet another knuckle where the steering column comes up to get your steering wheel to set at the right level. The U-joint-type knuckles cost around $50 each, so this setup won't be the best choice for saving a buck if you're on a budget.

The first setup I mentioned is way more cost effective, but it has one drawback: this particular setup is prone to bump-steer. Bump-steer is not fun, but a simple $40 steering damper will stop this from happening. If you weigh it out, one steering damper is cheaper than one knuckle U joint. It's your choice.

A few more pieces of advice: first, if given the choice between heim joints or tie rod ends for your pitman arm, drag links, and steering arm, it is to always wise to choose the heim joints because there is no slack in heim joints. The one place you don't want slack is in your steering. Ball joints will always allow you to turn the steering wheel some amount before the wheels turn. The tighter the system, the better your rod will handle.

Second, if you can't afford a steering damper, at least run a bar with heim joints on each end. One end mounts to the left side of the frame, and the other end mounts to the axle. It serves the same purpose as a pan hard bar in the rear and will cut down on sway. The ideal setup would be to use the pan hard bar and a steering damper, as this will give you a much better ride on those rough roads. If you have to cut costs, don't cut it on this part of the build.

One last thing: when installing your steering system, no matter which setup you use, think through every step. Be sure that you can dismantle the system as easily as you mounted it. You may decide that you're not happy with your box once you're driving your rod, necessitating a change. This is a good piece of advice for all of your builds; every piece should be able to be changed without a lot of trouble. Take your time and think the process through before you start welding.

PEDALS

Pedal to the metal is cool if you're talking gas pedal, but not so cool if you're talking brakes. It's time to tackle both along with the master cylinder. We found a gas pedal out of an S-10 Chevy and a brake pedal out of a GMC for $10 total. The brake pedal is massive in a rat rod, so we cut it down and refabbed it; quite a bit had to go. We got an M1930 master cylinder, which is very compact and lightweight. The best part: less than $20 at your local auto-parts store. With a piece of ¼-inch 4 × 4-inch plate, we scribed the outline of the master cylinder on it to locate the center hole and bolt pattern. We tacked this to the end of the bracket facing the firewall, transferred the holes onto the firewall with soap stone, and then drilled them out from the inside.

Next, we tacked our bracket to the dash and firewall after lining it up for best positioning. You need to consider your steering column and the clearance for your brake pedal. In our case, the pedal wouldn't work, so we cut all but 2 inches off of the pedal and added a piece of ¼-inch by ½-inch flat stock to the upper bracket. This gave us the right length and height off the floor. The pedal pad was kind of goofy, so we cut a Maltese cross out of a piece of ⅜-inch steel and tacked it on for position purposes. Once the pedal was in the right spot, we welded it solid.

The next issue was to fabricate a plunger. We measured from the master cylinder to the side peg on the pedal and made a plunger from a piece of ⅜-inch all-thread rod and a heavy washer. The end of the all-thread that goes into the master cylinder should be ground round for better connection. We tested to get maximum pedal travel for the plunger to bottom out. With everything working perfectly, we bolted up the master

cylinder and completed all welds. It helps to put a jack under your master cylinder to keep it level during all of these procedures.

The gas pedal was made to fit on the side of the trans tunnel, so that won't work for our application. We took the pedal rod and removed the bracket and pedal itself. The rod is boomerang-shaped, so that part is perfect; it just needed two L brackets welded to a 4 × 4-inch plate.

You will find that the end to which the pedal pad attaches will be about 1½ inches too long. Once you cut it, you can determine what to use for a pedal pad. Remember, think cheap! We welded two 1½-inch washers together and cut the shanks off two junk Phillips-head screwdrivers and, voilà, by welding the shanks in the center of the two washers (a figure 8, if you will), we had an early-Ford-V8-looking gas pedal. Our efforts gave us two pedal assemblies and a new master cylinder with washers and all-thread, all to the tune of around $30.

Now, onto the brake lines. Check your fitting sizes on the front brake hoses and rear end. You will need to get two adapters for your master cylinder so you can keep all of your fittings the same. If you don't have lines on your rear end, start there. A line from each rear hub to a T block attached to your rear end will work fine. Just remember to have a rubber brake hose into the third fitting of the T and then onto the brake line itself. This will allow travel of your rear end.

The brake line will go to the front fitting on your master cylinder: the front works the back brakes, and the back works the front brakes. Next, run a line from the back fitting to a T block on your left front frame rail. The left front brake hose fits into the second hole of the T and line out of the third over to your right front brake hose. Most parts houses carry a self-bleeder unit for about $10. You can bench-bleed your new master cylinder and bleed out your brake system alone in about twenty minutes.

As for your brake lines, you can buy a bending kit and make all of your own bends to fit your situation, or you can buy prefitted lines and screw them together. Just get all of your measurements and buy your lines accordingly. You will seldom hear me say "new" anything, but my one exception is brakes. Don't chance an old, worn-out master cylinder or lines. This is one of the most critical parts of your rod, so don't cut pennies here.

MOUNTS

If you've built your own frame, as we discussed, you should have a couple of short pieces of your 2 × 3 × ⅛-inch wall thickness rectangular tubing left over. If not, find some at your local scrap yard. These serve great as your base. You can get the motor mounts from mid-'70s through mid-'80s trucks pretty cheap and have some cushion to prevent vibration.

A 45-degree cut on one end of your tubing will mount to the inside of your frame, and the other end will weld to your motor mount. Things to consider are, number one, motor height. The higher your motor sits, the less chance you have of ever dragging your oil pan. Number two, the higher the motor sits, the more commanding it looks. We've all seen a small block dwarfed by what looks like a monster radiator grill and tall firewall. The motor gets lost in the shuffle. There's something extremely cool about driving your rod down the road and looking out at your manifold and carb. Better still is to see your valve covers, too. You may say that that sounds freaky, and I say exactly! It's a rat rod. The freakier, the better.

There's something else to consider. Your drive shaft has to run at least 3 degrees in pitch and 6 degrees maximum. Six degrees is pretty major and will accommodate your high-sitting block unless your rear end is pointed downward. If your rear end is pointed 3 degrees up or your motor is 3 degrees down, it still is within tolerance. A $10 degree finder will settle all of this. The main thing is to not have less than 3 degrees and not have more than 6 degrees of pitch. A half bubble on a 4-foot level will also indicate 3–5 degrees of pitch.

Don't be afraid to play with all of this. It's only metal—it recuts and rewelds, and no one's keeping tabs. The right end result is all that you are after. Now would also be a good time for painting and dressing up your motor before it goes in. A $20 set of tall valve covers would also be a nice touch to give some mass to the motor. You can tell that I grew up in the "Big Daddy Roth" era: big motor, tall shifter, big back tires … you get the picture.

The next thing to work on is your trans mount. A tab welded on each side of the frame and a piece of 3 × ¼-inch strap works well. You can bolt the trans mount to the strap and the strap to the two tabs, and you're done. This will make it easy to remove if you ever need to.

MOUNTS

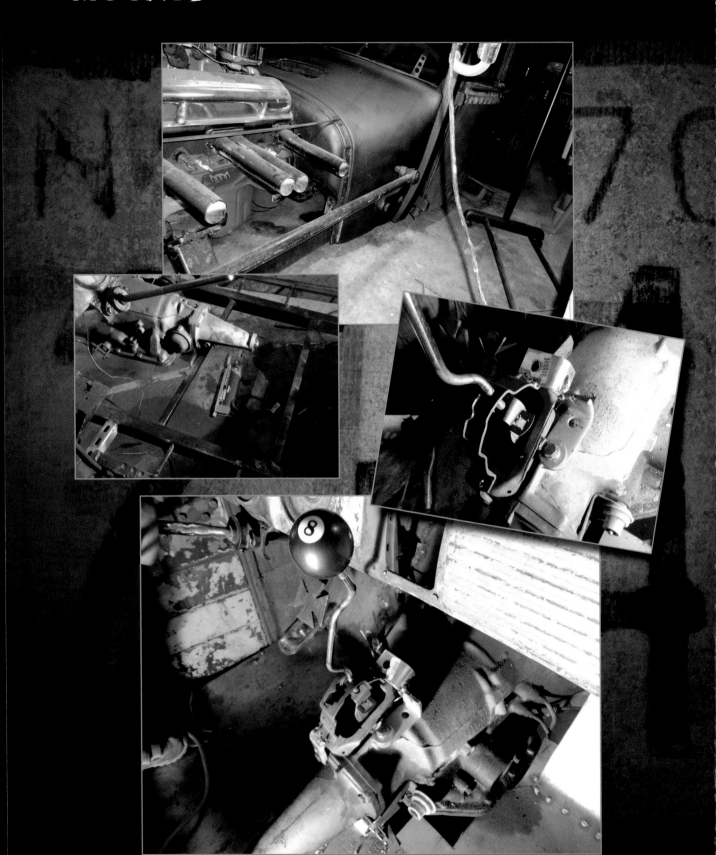

After this comes the drive shaft. Hopefully, you got a drive shaft with the trans you bought. The yoke that fits your rear end (whichever one you use) and the trans yoke can be coupled together by a job-shop-type machine shop. A drive-shaft-cutting business will cost you more than a mom-and-pop machine shop. I was paying $150 until I tried a small machine shop, and now I get the two yokes coupled to my existing tube—cut, fit, and balanced—for $50. The key is to have a tube, even if it's not the right one. The shop can cut the old yokes off and mount yours on.

Here again—shop, shop, shop. Don't take the first price until you know it's the cheapest price. The prices will vary big time from shop to shop. Or, if you are handy with a chop saw and a mig, you can do it yourself and have it balanced by someone else.

Now we are ready for a shifter. The possibilities are endless. You can find shifters at swap meets for anywhere from $10 to $150, you can pull one from a junk car at a scrap yard for around $25, or you can get creative and make one from an old tractor lever or emergency-brake handle or whatever your mind dreams up. One option to consider is using a three- or four-speed stick shift and cutting the back leg off. The front leg will allow you to get all of the gears in an automatic trans one click at a time.

At swap meets, the Hurst shifters go high, but the old off-brand shifters, and especially the three-speeds, go dirt cheap, usually between $10 and $20. You can cut them and extend them as tall as you want, but the main thing is that your linkage is already there with an arm, brackets, and everything to be hooked up. There are no cables or trying to figure how to hook it to your trans lever. It's all there. Just a thought.

THE GRILLE

The first impression of your rod will be what people see as you approach them on the road or as they approach you at a show. The grille, radiator, headlights, and overall look of the front of your rod set the tone for your audience. One major turnoff is when the radiator and grille sit higher than the cowl. Another is when the headlights are too far away from the grille. I've seen rods with headlights 16 inches away from the grille, and it looks freaky, even by rat rod standards. Thus, we will discuss some techniques that will help you put your best foot forward. The first step is to decide on the best radiator for the job at the lowest cost.

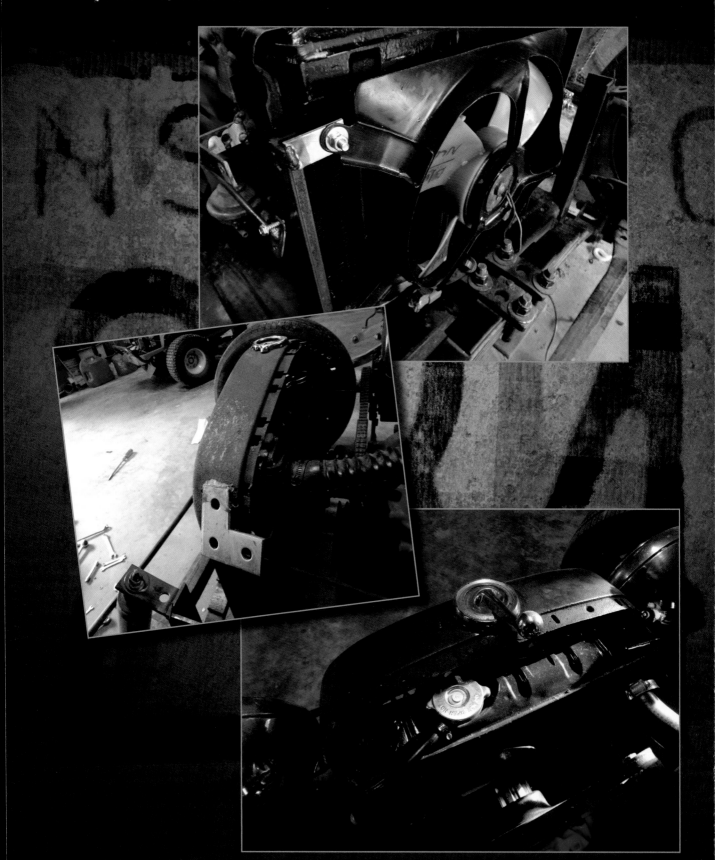

Most '20s and '30s radiator grilles are very narrow and not very tall, so that rules out many radiators that would otherwise work. Most small foreign-car radiators would work except for the fact that they won't cool a V8 motor. That brings us to '64 through '66 Mustang radiators. They're the perfect height and width to fit inside vintage grilles, and if you choose the ones out of the V8 Mustangs, they will easily cool other V8s as well. These radiators can be found from $20 to $75 at swap meets or at less than $150 new from an auto parts store.

Start by getting two pieces of 3-foot-long ¾ × ¾-inch angle iron. Measure the length of your bolt holes and cut the steel to that height. Center the radiator on the front of the frame, mark where the angle needs to set to be welded to the frame, and line your marks up with the bolt patterns on the radiator. Remember to set the radiator on the inside of the front frame and slide it down until the top is below the cowl. Allow a little room because the grille will shroud the radiator and stand a little taller. A 4-foot level will tell you when the top of the grille and the cowl are lined up. Tack on the angle iron, check the alignment again, and then weld it solid with two small gussets for stability.

Drill your bolt-pattern holes and bolt the radiator to the angle iron. If you're going to install an electric fan, now is the time to do so. If you plan to mount it in front of the radiator, it's as simple as holding the fan up, marking where it will sit against the two angle irons, and welding the tabs on the front side of the angle.

With the radiator and fan mounted, it's time to mount your radiator grille. Once it is in position, mark where you will weld two L brackets to the side of the grille at the bottom, and screw two self-tappers to the other side of the L onto the frame. L-bracket the top from the shell to the backside of the same angle iron that's holding the radiator in place. Enough of your radiator will be sticking out in back of the grille to easily get to your cap and all hose fittings.

There are several options for headlights. Shown on page 186 are a set of $5 chrome buckets from a swap meet so priced because the side of each is rusted out. We simply turned the buckets sideways and mounted them to a bracket welded to the sides of the grille. To see the rust, you would have to lie on your back—besides, these are rat rods. Rust is cool, remember?

Another rod we have has a tractor grille, which lent itself to bolting the headlights the same way (sideways) directly onto the tractor grille. Just remember to turn your headlight lenses

THE GRILLE

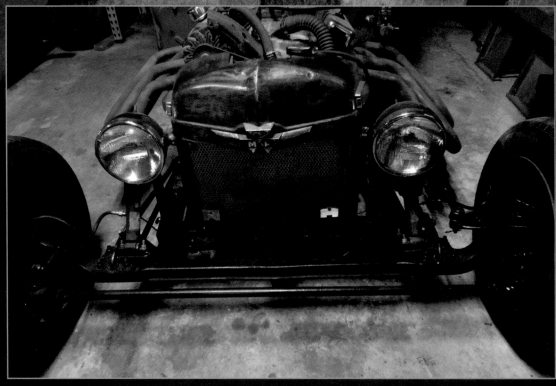

up and down because they otherwise create a funky light pattern and are not nearly as bright. The third type of headlight mount we will cover is to simply cut a piece of 2 × 2-inch angle iron the length from the frame to midway up on the grille. You can cap it on top for your headlights to sit on, and it will also serve as a bracket to which your front shocks mount. A small gusset welded to the bottom backside onto the frame will provide all the strength you will need to pull this off.

The inside of the angle iron also serves as a great place to hide your headlight wires so they won't be seen from the front or side of the rod. In the case of the wires mounted to the grille itself, they can be hidden inside the grille, running down to the frame. Next, to hide the ugly fan showing through the front of your grille, you can buy a sheet of steel mesh from your home-supply store, found in the department where outdoor grills are sold. It is a single piece of mesh wrapped in cardboard, and it's the perfect size to fit inside the grille front and hide all the mess—all for around $15. It can be bolted in or tack-welded if you don't mind pulling the whole grille when the fan goes out. Either way, it's a cool look at a cheap price.

WIRING

There's nothing that will inspire you like the moment that you get your rod wired and fired up for the first time. You may have just heard the same motor run in the vehicle you pulled it from, but I can promise you that it's a totally different ball game when you hear it in your very own hand-built rat rod. It all starts with your decision about which wiring kit to use. I've used several different kits, and I must say that they're very similar to install, but the prices vary quite a bit. The cheaper kits work just as well, so why spend the extra money?

Wiring kits are divided into three sections: one to the back, one to the dash, and one to the motor and front section. The directions spell out everything a first-timer needs to know, so I won't waste space with details other than to suggest that you do yourself a favor and wire a toggle-switch light above your fuse box. In a perfect world, everyone would carry a flashlight. In a perfect world, fuses would never blow—but since they do, and usually on a dark road, a light above your fuse box under your dash will be a lifesaver.

My only other tip is to use rubber bushings on all metal holes that your wires go through. Rat rods vibrate, and I can promise that it will wear a naked place on a wire somewhere, and you'll end up talking nasty to your rat rod.

On to your dashboard. You can find a variety of dashboards at swap meets anywhere from $50 to $200. In our case, we decided to keep the same dash to save money, but because all of the gauges were junk, we changed the gauge clusters. A 1949 Chevy truck has two fairly large clusters, so we tacked metal onto the right one and cut the left one out to fit a 1953 Ford panel that we bought for $10 at a swap meet.

We used the cluster as a pattern to trace around and cut to fit. A little Bondo to hide the plate tacked into the hole and filler for the ashtray and walls, and, voilà—it looks like it was meant for this truck. Since the '53 Ford was 6-volt, we swapped panel lights with 12-volt sockets that you can get at a parts store for a few dollars each. The speedo is mechanical, so it didn't matter. You will replace your other gauges with mechanical ones as well to keep the wiring simple.

On the same subject is your power source. The ideal spot for the battery on these trucks is in the truck bed. We found a spot in the center of the frame with plenty of clearance to allow the rear end its up-and-down motion. We also made sure that it did not to ride so high as to hit the deck lid, causing a problem short. The battery also serves as great weight distribution right where you need it over the back tires. We used our battery as a pattern to attach the back corners and sides to support the battery. Each piece was tacked only and fitted each time with the battery for clearance.

Once everything fit right, we made solid welds and welded a thick washer to the frame to connect a strap from the back to the front to hold the battery in place on those rough roads and curves. It costs less to buy a section of heavy-gauge wire and make up your own cables than to buy premade cables. In the first place, it's hard to find a premade cable to run from the extreme back of your rod all the way to the front. Even if you do, it will cost you dearly.

The next step before firing it up is the gas tank. Of course, you can buy a store-bought fuel cell, but because we're doing low-budget, here are some points to ponder. One low-dollar idea is a Model H Farmall tractor tank. The tank sits flat on the tractor, but it can be turned onto its side and slid down between the rear end and back frame. You only need to block your existing filler and supply holes and retack them into the edge, which is now the top. It's the perfect height, width, and thickness for the application.

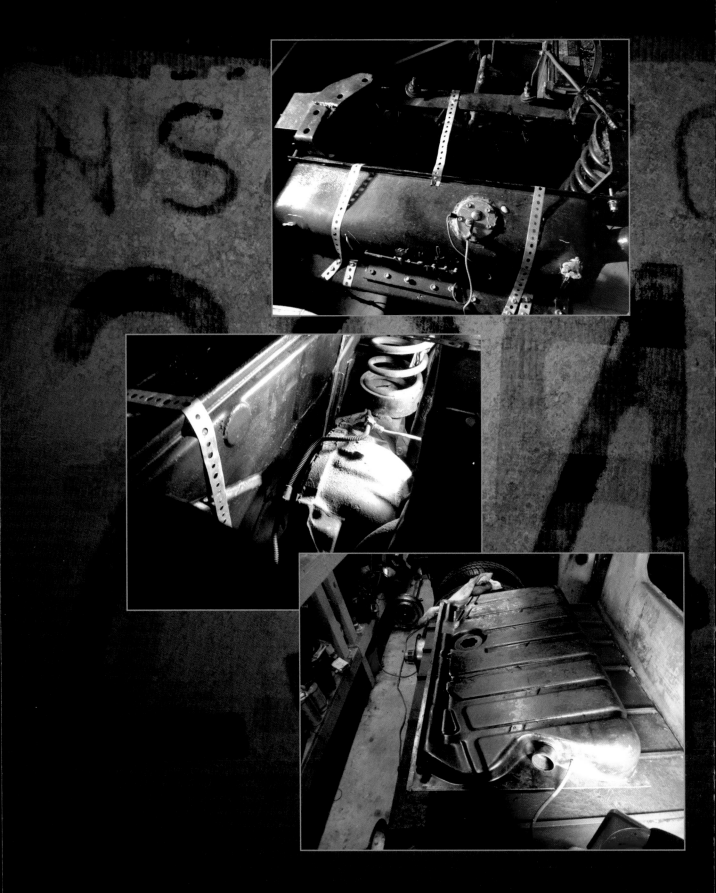

Another choice is any of the small truck tanks from the early models. The one pictured is from a Chevy LUV truck, and, as you can see, it fits perfectly between the frame rails and is a good height to be hidden by your deck lid. Recycle yards require car owners to remove the gas tanks, so I see heaps of gas tanks piled up. You can search through these and often find a winner. If there is mild rust in the tank, you can soak it with one part molasses and nine parts water for a day or so, and it will totally clear up all of the rust. For light rust, apple cider vinegar will work, but molasses is the key for heavier rust. Once the rust is gone, you can use a rust sealer in the tank to prevent it from coming back.

After searching for a tank for our '49 Chevy truck project, we found a '74 Volkswagen gas tank that fits like a glove. It fits great between the frame rails, is not too wide, and is just the right thickness as well.

The tank is made on an angle, but the top sits flat, so the only kicker is to run the side frame from 4 inches in the back to nothing in the front. The gas outlet sits at the right front, which makes it easy because most fuel pumps are on the right anyway. To hide all of these components is as easy as a sheet of 18- to 22-gauge steel. You can tack a piano hinge to the front and the cab and simply hood-pin the back to keep it from rattling on bumpy roads. A cheap hardware handle to lift it with, and you're in business.

FINISHING TOUCHES

We've come to the end of our promised $1,500 rat rod build. You now have a street-legal, true-blue driving rod that's ready for the road. This is just the beginning because you can go out and have a ball! You can sell the rod and make a nice profit, or you can keep tweaking until it is a street rod. It's your choice, and that's what I love about America.

Now I want to show how we came up with the price tag. The truck cab was $300, and the steel to build the frame was about $100, but steel prices have come down since that time; I bought just enough steel at a steel mill to start my next rod, and it was $59. The straight axle from a '68 Dodge truck was $100 and the Dodge van rear end was $50. The motor, trans, and driveshaft came from a wrecked '82 Chevy truck, which also provided pedals, belts, hoses, clamps, lightbulbs, cables, nuts and bolts, a wiring harness, and many other parts, all of which cost $500. I sold the rear end

FINISHING TOUCHES

for $100 to buy the $50 Dodge rear end to keep the bolt pattern the same as the Dodge straight axle. This sounds crazy, but when you have a flat, which you will, and you have only one spare, it needs to fit anywhere on the rod.

We are rodders, so we need to be practical. To save time, I bought a $120 harness online and put the '82 Chevy harness back for another build. The grille shell, steering box, shifter, light buckets, and radiator were all swap-meet finds totaling $120. By the way, when you buy multiple things from the same person at a swap meet, the price goes down drastically; if you buy them late in the day, at the end of the swap meet, even more so. The '53 Ford instrument panel was also a swap-meet find for $10, and the stock Dodge steel wheels totaled $40. We saved the wheels and tires from the '82 Chevy truck for another build and bought four used tires for a total of $100.

The seats came from a school-supply and furniture business that sells used school chairs for $10 each. The gauges came from a swap meet for $20. Finally, the windshield—the windshield on a '49 Chevy truck is simply two pieces of flat glass. You will save a fortune by making your own pattern from a piece of stiff cardboard and shopping glass cutters. If you buy a piece of safety glass, almost any glass company will cut it for you. Our windshield turned out to be $50, bringing us to $1,480. This leaves you $20 to buy your scrap 18-gauge sheet metal to build the bed with, and you're at $1,500, as promised, with some leftover parts for the next build—and that's how it's done!

TIME TO DRIVE

Now we'll move on to getting your rod legal and on the street. Most of these $300 to $500 cars or bodies will not have titles. That's no problem, but do make sure that you get a bill of sale with a name and address. That will go a long way with your local license agent. You can apply for a lost title, but it will come back with the previous owner's name, and then you'll have to track down all of that information. If the serial number is gone, and it

Negotiating

This would be a good time to stop and explain some business dealings. When you walk into a used tire store or a swap meet, have only the amount you want to spend in your wallet. Don't say, "How much for these tires?" Instead, say, "I have only $100, and I want to buy these four tires." Open your wallet and show your money. This is a toss of the coin, but I can tell you that it works more often than not. Just because someone gives you a price doesn't mean that's what you're going to pay; it's only a starting point for bartering.

probably will be on these old vehicles, you can take the number off the motor block you're using. This, with the bill of sale, will get you a title in your name.

Another option is to buy a title at a swap meet or car show. These are titles of vehicles that have been crushed and no longer exist. They sell for $50 to $150 for most old 1940s, '50s, and '60s vehicles. You can buy a VIN tag and have the bought title number put on it at most mall engraving booths. If your rod is in the 1920s or '30s, the titles are very expensive, and you're better off using your bill of sale with a block serial number.

The final option is to keep all of your receipts from the build and call your local theft-recovery government office. They will send out an agent to inspect what you have built and issue a new title. The only thing I don't like about doing it this way is that your title will say the current year, not the year of the vehicle. This sucks when you go to sell it and the title for your 1946 Ford says "2014 homemade vehicle." This is a turnoff to me, but it's up to you.

Finally, if at all possible, get an antique vehicle tag. An antique tag costs one-third of what a regular tag costs, and you don't have to renew it every year. The tag stays with the vehicle and can't be transferred, but for the price, who cares? In our state, an antique plate costs $17 and a regular plate costs $60. It's a pretty easy choice for me. Antique tags are for recreational purposes, and that's exactly what we are using them for.

Insurance, through a car-collector-type agent, will be very inexpensive. I pay $250 a year for full coverage up to $10,000 replacement. It covers everything that other policies cover, plus free towing and other bonuses. The thing I love most is that in case of fire, theft, wreck, or whatever, you get a check for $10,000—no appraisals, no questions asked. If you're driving a rat rod, this is an ideal policy.

I want to finish by thanking all of you who have followed this build and are loyal to *Rat Rod Magazine*. It is our goal to do our best to help you in your goal, and that goal is to build and live in this rat rod world that we love so much. My heart goes out to the guy fighting to put food on the table and juggling a rod build at the same time. Keep working that dream, and it will happen.

Rat Rod Magazine's
Tour Rat Builds

Rat Rod Magazine's head builder, Bryan Dagel, has made a habit of building with durability and safety in mind. With the *Rat Rod* flagship vehicles, we've had to put an emphasis on the quality of workmanship to serve as an example for young or new builders. The following build recaps showcase Bryan's approach to building these vehicles for the Rat Rod Tour.

2011 TOUR RAT BUILD

The build for the 2011 Tour Rat began with some artist's sketches and rough ideas, as most builds do. We were initially going to use a '29 Chevy sedan body, but when Matt Petrovic, a member of the Peckerheadz Car Club in Minnesota, offered up this '31 DeSoto body, we quickly shifted gears. The cost of the body? Some magazines.

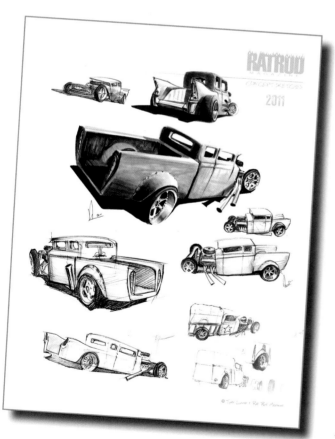

We shortened the DeSoto body from a four-door to a two-door. One of the doors was missing some skin, so Bryan cannibalized one of the other doors, and we ended up with a complete body. The five-window style gives us a little extra leg room. The vision, inspired by the body, was something like this: the DeSoto will be chopped a few inches and channeled 6 inches. The bed will be fabricated using the rear end of a 1960 Plymouth wagon and fitted with a functional trunk. The engine will be an SBC 350—built for durability while retaining a little pop. The tranny will be a 700R4. All of this will set on a modified S-10 frame. And then the build began.

Thanks to help from Shapiro Steel, we were able to secure enough expanded steel to deck out the entire interior for a sturdy industrial look. Bryan said it best: "People are going to know we have a steel sponsor."

My favorite part of the build aesthetically is the sweet '34 Hudson Terraplane grille and headlight set that Bryan found on eBay. It was a bit too tall and long for the project but fit perfectly after a little fiery persuasion.

Our friends at Mora Motorworks built the Tour Rat's engine. These guys built us something that is efficient, durable, and a perfect fit for our "drive it hard, drive it far" concept.

Once the body was shortened and the door repaired, as previously mentioned, our focus shifted to the frame. The frame was an early 1990s S-10 that had to be pinched 20 inches in the front in so that the DeSoto body would fit on it. Bryan's dad, Larry, used thick-wall 2 × 3-inch tubing. It took a couple of days for Larry to trim and tweak the frame to where we needed it. We then hauled the frame back to Bryan's shop, where we fitted it with some temporary wheels.

Bryan quickly took to the torch to cut off all of the extra GM mounting material. When the frame was cleaned up enough, the body was set to measure for channeling. We wanted a low, mean stance, so Bryan cut about 6 inches to the lower firewall mounts to get the body lower on the frame and then sliced out the same amount on the back of the cab. The body was still braced up from the earlier sectioning/shortening, so we set the body on the frame and got her down real low. Next came a bunch of welding. Bryan set the body up on three individual cross-braces using 1 × 2-inch thick-wall tubing: two braces at the door openings front and rear and one brace across the glass section. Bryan then made a perimeter around the body's interior flooring with 1 × 1-inch tubing; he calls this a "crash zone" around the people sitting inside. We used eight mounting bolts on ½-inch rubber pads to keep her on the frame safely. Bryan recommends using at least six because he'd hate to have the body come off the frame in an accident; he cautions builders to "bolt it down good!" The next step was to figure out where to place the seat and seat-belt bracing. At that point, we were still waiting for our seats, so Bryan just went ahead and sheeted the floor in 20-gauge steel without welding it down until we could decide on the placement.

From there, Bryan started working on the radiator/grille mounting. We used a really nice shorty aluminum radiator from Dillon Radiators that fit the car beautifully. We used a chunk of 3 × 3-inch angle iron to tie the frame horns together at the proper height to set the radiator in. The radiator sat just a little lower than the cowl, so our Terraplane grille slid right over, also at the proper height. Bryan set the matching Hudson headlights up so we could stare at it—and it looked great.

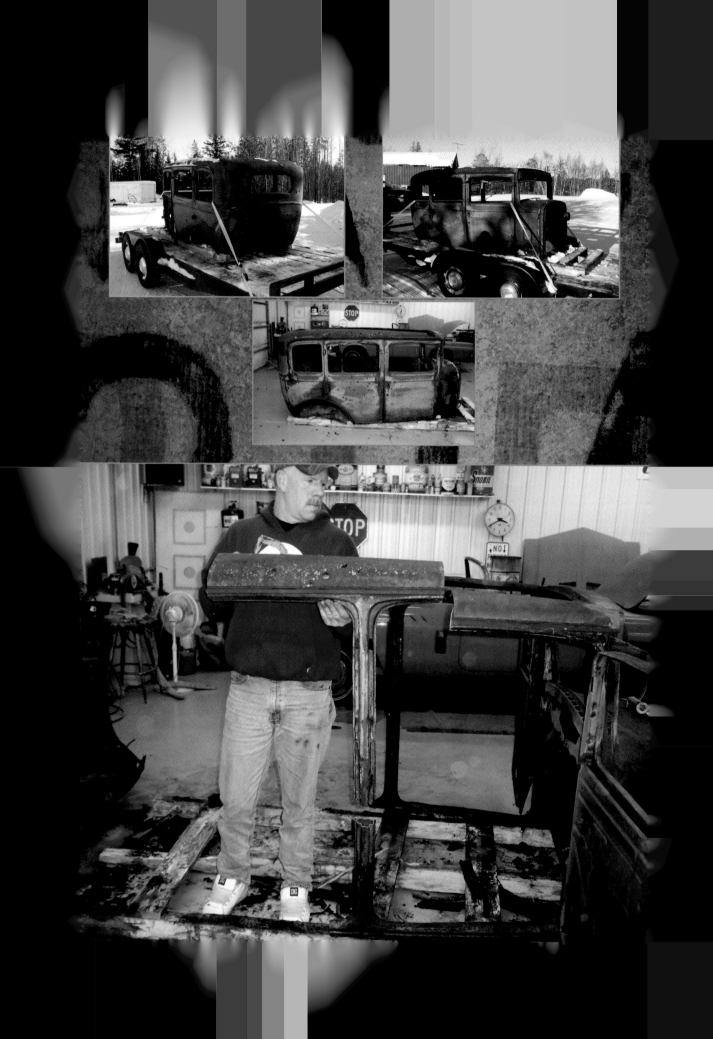

The frame horns looked like crap, so Bryan pie-cut them and welded plate across to close them up. This helped aesthetically and worked well with the industrial theme of the project.

Next, Bryan pulled up the 1960 Plymouth wagon donor car and began to prep it for the cut. He had to pull the rear glass to get enough of the quarters to work with. Then came out Bryan's other best friend, the Sawzall! After a few minutes of cutting, we had the quarter skins off and were working on pulling the tailgate.

Bryan then dove into the interior, where we pillaged the dash for its speedo cluster, which we thought was extremely cool. All of this cannibalism left the old Plymouth looking pretty sick but well worth the parts we needed to make a box for the Tour Rat. By the time Bryan got the wagon cut, right-hand-man Dave Novy had the panels for the front fabricated, so we got those welded in, which really cleaned up the nose. We then shifted our focus back to the box—a lot of 1 × 2-inch steel tubing to make the floor frame and mounting points. Again, we bolted it down good. We used six bolts to tighten down the framework to the truck frame. We then mocked up them bad-ass quarter fins. With a little creative thinking, we came up with a decent (safe) way to pull this off.

Next up was the tailgate. We had to narrow the gate about 26 inches to fit the rear of the truck, so, unfortunately, there will be no functioning tailgate. After we got it tacked together, we started fabbing the inside of the box. We used a lot of 20-gauge sheeting with tons of plug welds to give us the industrial look we were going for. We put all of that Shapiro steel to good use! Before we tacked the inners in the box, we had to make a gas filler tube to dump the gas into our modified S-10 gas tank. We used the wagon's stock gas filler/cap position in the quarter panels to keep her clean-looking, and then we welded up the inner box, again with a lot of plug welds. When we were satisfied with the box, we turned our attention to the interior. The FedEx man had shown up with a set of bad-ass bomber seats.

We jumped into the interior and started mocking up the placement of the important stuff, such as the brake-pedal assembly and the steering column. We cut a hole in the firewall and made an interior dash mount for the column and then got the brake assembly mounted in. Remember that wherever you mount that brake assembly, it has to be thick enough to take the pedal pressure. It would be a tragedy to hit the brakes and have them fold under the pressure of your foot and crash in a ball of flames, so it's important to do it right the first time. Bryan set the column in place, bolted it in, and connected the steering shaft to the steering box. It worked great. We checked out the seat placement and then mounted the shifter. Bryan used a B&M shifter with a neutral safety switch. Don't kid yourself; they do work and keep your rod from running off while starting. The interior came together decently, and the placement wasn't too bad. It's comfortable to drive with a ton of leg room. Keep in mind that this is a channeled rod, and you normally lose a lot of room with the channel. We were able to keep it comfy while still maintaining that low, aggressive look.

Next, we jumped back to the box. We had to pull it off so we had room to cut the top. After placing the seats in the car, we decided that 3 inches is all that we would dare cut out. We wanted to have nice sight lines and good visibility so we could drive this thing comfortably, so we taped up 3-inch strips and busted out the Sawzall again.

A little cutting here and there, and we were ready to place the top back on. We had to fill in a few gunshot wounds to the windshield pillars in the process. The chop helped with the proportions of the car, giving it a "meaner" look. Again, a lot of welding to get it right. Then Bryan fabbed up some roof braces to match the crown of the roof and welded them in. At this point, the Tour Rat was really taking shape. We had the doors off when we cut the roof, so we had to finish the cut on the doors and then reinstall them, which helped a lot. With the cab just about complete, we bounced back to the box and rear bumper. We also had to narrow the rear bumper by 26 inches to get the right fit. The work became a blur, jumping back and forth from end to end, trying to finish up everything by the deadline. We got everything wired and tied up all of the loose ends, along with the aesthetic touches (decals, pinstriping, etc.). And a 1931 DeSoto rat rod was born.

2012 TOUR RAT BUILD

The vision for the 2012 Tour Rat started with a '36 Chevy panel body that was wasting away at our friend Roger Rentola's house up in Barnum, Minnesota. (I say it was wasting away, while Roger would probably tell you that he was just about to pull it out of the snowbank and start building. Either way—he gave it up, and we couldn't have been happier.) With more weight to push around than the previous year, we needed to up the ante in several areas of the build: bigger engine, stronger structure, and some extra attention to the brakes and mechanical systems.

The following is adapted from Bryan Dagel's 2012 build journal.

Well, it's that time of the year here in Minnesota … brrrrrr. Time to start on the 2012 *Rat Rod Magazine* Tour Rat. This year's build isn't going to be as out-of-the-box as last year's build. This year, we'll start with a 1936 Chevy panel truck that we found in Mahtowa, Minnesota. Roger Rentola picked up the panel on the way to the junkyard back in the '90s and set it aside for a future project. Well, time rolled by, and there it sat. I saw the panel while at Roger's and thought that it would be a good touring truck— plenty of room for garb.

2012 TOUR RAT BUILD

First off is the frame. We were going to go old-school, but, as in rat rodding, money came into play, so we settled on the reliable S-10 frame. The parts are so affordable that we couldn't pass it up. Had to pinch the first 33 inches of the frame to get the panel body on. Also had to stretch it 4 inches to match the panel's original wheelbase. So, once that was buttoned up, we went to mount the body, which fit like a glove over the freshly pinched and stretched frame. A few body mounts, and we were in business. Next up was the huge panel body. I thought that sectioning and chopping would do this big truck justice. I'm telling you now that it's easier to build it in your head first rather than just start cutting it up and finding yourself in quicksand. Tape is your best friend when it comes to cutting up something like this. Take your time and think it through before cutting into the rig!

Once you think you have it, start cutting. I decided to section the body 3 inches, cut out 2 inches, and overlap 1 inch into the lower body section—the rear half first, then the middle, and then the windshield portion. Every time you lower a part of the truck, it must grow longer to keep up with the lower section, so we made two cuts from drip rail to drip rail to stretch out the roof. These were used on the section and also the chop top. Once the section and chop were completed, we could patch up the roof with a filler strip. When the sectioning was completed, I mocked up running boards and front fenders. The chop came later, when I had a few guys to help hold the roof. As I mocked up front end, David Novy welded up the bracing for the floors inside the truck. We had to burn the candle at both ends to get this done on time. Panel was really looking good; sectioning helped the overall look of the truck. I couldn't wait to chop this!

Next, I was off to pick up our rebuilt Vortec 350 and tranny and set them in and see how they fit. The motor had to slide back a few inches to fit it all under a hood.

This Tour Rat build produced a truly dependable machine. It tackled the Rocky Mountains, deserts, Route 66, the frozen North Country—and anything else we threw at it.

Although we won't publish the entire build documentation here, hopefully this excerpt based on Bryan's journal will help capture some of the vision behind it. A builder should plan and plan again before making critical cuts and decisions.

2013 TOUR RAT BUILD

The year after the panel build, Bryan embarked on a journey to push the envelope in creating the 2013 Tour Rat. The 2011 build had been quite a talker with those 1960 Plymouth wings on the bed, so in 2013—after building the much more traditional Chevy panel—Bryan returned to the winged-bed concept and once again merged two iconic cars. This time, Bryan took the shell of a 1937 Lincoln Zephyr that was destined for the crusher and transformed what was left of it into a pickup cab. The Zephyr body is very round, almost Volkswagen-like when stripped down, so it took some foresight to make it look right. The bed was crafted from an old decrepit 1957 Chevy Bel Air wagon, similar to the DeSoto that Bryan had built in 2011.

While that mating of two bodies was similar, the engine was not. Instead of a small-block Chevy 350, the Zephyr would house a 455 Oldsmobile Rocket big block. We weren't looking for gas mileage with this one; we wanted more of an earth-rattler. This Tour Rat also had an old-school front suspension (no IFS this time) and was airbagged so we could set it down on the ground at shows.

Once again, Bryan had put together a solid machine. Like those he had built before it, this one did not have a single breakdown. Ever.

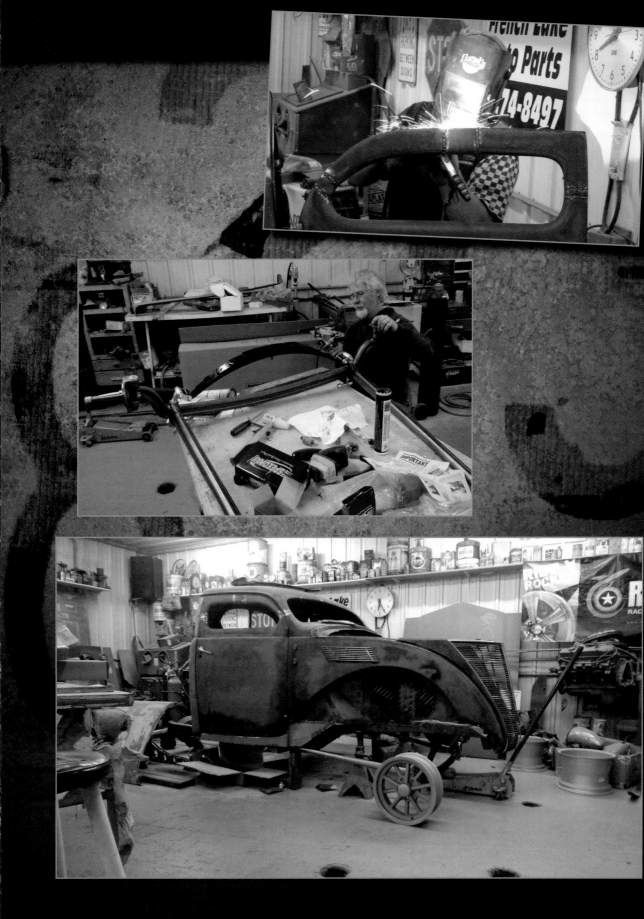

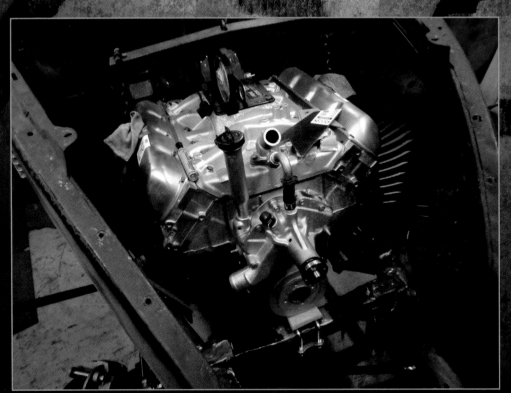

2015 TOUR RAT BUILD

Staying true to the dependable, extremely drivable Tour Rat lineage, Bryan Dagel took the latest *Rat Rod Magazine* build back to its blue-collar roots. It's a 1935 Chevy sitting atop a beautiful custom frame, with a slight steampunk flavor to it—but definitely delivering a more traditional rat rod look than its predecessors.

Because it's common, inexpensive, and provides the dependability, easy access to parts, and decent gas mileage we need for long drives, this build will be powered by a 350 sbc crate motor. Pairing it up with a 700r4 transmission gives us that overdrive for the highway, and still has the pop to burn those back tires if we want.

This car will be showcased at the SEMA Show in Las Vegas, Nevada—the country's largest automotive trade show—later in 2015. With SEMA in mind, it is important to Bryan and *Rat Rod Magazine* that the car represent rat rod culture as a whole—something that is hard to accomplish with just one vehicle—but a challenge Bryan has accepted. There are elements of a budget build and elements of a high-end rat rod. It stays true to blue-collar hot rodding while utilizing modern technologies like the ESTOPP electric E-brake and other features. The body is prototypical rat rod, but with a more elaborate frame design and some other cool features that have yet to be implemented. There won't be much shine to it, but there will be plenty of high-quality craftsmanship.

The concept drawing for 2015's *Rat Rod Magazine* Tour Rat.

Rat Rod Terminology

409: Top Chevrolet engine option from 1961 to 1965. Immortalized in the Beach Boys' song titled "409."

art car: Automobile that has been created, modified, altered, or otherwise customized by using the vehicle as a canvas to display an artist's expression.

artillery wheels: Nickname given to scalloped steel wheels similar to those used on artillery vehicles during World War I.

bagged: Vehicle that utilizes airbags instead of shock absorbers, leaf springs, coils, and the like to control both ride comfort and height.

BBC: Abbreviation for "big block Chevy," a larger-displacement engine produced by Chevrolet. Common sizes (in cubic-inch displacement): 396, 402, 427, and 454. Also known as a "rat" motor, regardless of whether or not it is used in a rat rod.

belly tanker: Early style of hot rod constructed from the auxiliary fuel tank of a P-38 aircraft used in World War II. The cheap price and aerodynamic efficiency of the tanks made them very popular on dry lake beds of Southern California. Also called "lakesters."

big and littles: Practice of using much larger wheels and tires on the rear of a vehicle as compared to the front.

billet: Generally refers to any block of metal; in the hot-rod world, it refers to aluminum alloy used in a plethora of applications, from engine parts to interior pieces and wheels. It is normally shunned in the rat-rod community for its shine and expense, but its use in the rat-rod world has gained some support.

blower: Slang term for a supercharger, which is a mechanically driven air compressor that increases the density or pressure of air supplied to an engine.

blue oval: Blue, oval-shaped insignia of Ford Motor Company; colloquial nickname for any Ford product.

bomb: Pre-1960 lowrider car or truck.

bomber seat: Seat designed to look like those utilized in World War II bomber planes.

booger weld: Derogatory term to describe a poorly executed weld.

camshaft: Eccentric metal shaft in an engine that determines when the intake and exhaust valves open and close.

carburetor: Part that regulates the flow of fuel and air in an engine via engine vacuum.

channel: To drop the body of a car or truck over the frame to reduce overall height.

cheater slick: Racing tire with a completely smooth, or "slick," surface except for the most minimal of tread, often consisting of a single groove around the circumference of the surface.

chop: Removing pieces of the roof and/or roof pillars to lower the profile of the vehicle.

Cleveland: Series of Ford small-block engines made primarily in a plant in Cleveland, Ohio. Common displacements (in cubic inches): 302, 351, 400.

COE (cab over engine): Utility truck design in which the cab is placed directly over the engine.

crankshaft: Mechanical part of an engine that converts the reciprocal motion of the moving pistons into rotational motion, which powers the vehicle.

Cummins: Brand of diesel engine found in many Dodge ¾-ton and 1-ton pickups; these and have become very popular as power plants for rat rods.

Dearborn: Michigan city where Ford Motor Company was founded.

deck: Removing the chrome trim from the trunk of a vehicle.

deuce: Any reference to a 1932 Ford coupe or roadster. The 1932 Ford is considered by many to be the perfect foundation for the start of any hot-rod build.

diamond tuck: Type of upholstery pattern in which the stitching is run at (or near) 90-degree angles over heavy padding, and then the upholstery itself is turned 90 degrees. The result is that the design appears as diamond shapes instead of squares.

disc brake: Type of brake that uses calipers to squeeze pairs of pads against a disc in order to create friction. More efficient with regard to cooling and resistance to fade as compared to drum brakes.

doodlebug: Term used to describe a tractor or other motorized farm vehicle made from an older vehicle, generally a Ford Model T. In many cases, it was more economical to create a doodlebug than buy an actual tractor.

drop axle: Front axle that has been modified in order to lower the front end of a vehicle. The ends of the axle are heated, and the axle is reshaped using a press, metalworking tools, or both. Drop axles are now usually purchased instead of being created manually.

drop spindle: Wheel spindle that has been modified to center the wheel higher on the spindle in order to lower the front of the vehicle.

drum brake: Type of brake that uses friction caused by a set of shoes or pads that press against a rotating drum. Less efficient with regard to cooling and resistance to fade as compared to disc brakes.

dry lake: Location (usually in Southern California) where drag racing got its start. Dried-up lakes provided a smooth, uninterrupted surface that allowed competitors to run their cars at top speed without having to worry about things like traffic, pedestrians, and the like.

dual exhausts: Exhaust system terminating with an exhaust pipe exiting from beneath each side of the vehicle. A true dual exhaust consists of an exhaust pipe coming from each bank of cylinders.

Duramax: Diesel engine found in many General Motors ¾-ton and 1-ton pickups. These engines have become very popular as power plants for rat rods.

FE-engine: Series of Ford big-block engines. Common displacements (in cubic inches): 352, 390, 410, 427, 428.

flathead: Engine design in which the valves reside in the block rather than in the head. Ford's flathead V-8 revolutionized the early days of high-performance automobiles because of its adaptability to tuning tricks and its high (for the day) torque and horsepower output.

four link: Type of rear suspension that is designed to locate the rear axle with four links, two on each side.

french: Customizing technique in which an external assembly such as a headlight, taillight, or antenna is recessed into the body, usually seamlessly.

fuel injected: Method of delivering the fuel/air mixture into an engine. It is different from carburetion in that carburetion utilizes engine vacuum to draw in the mixture, while fuel injection utilizes high pressure to atomize the mixture and force it into the engine.

gennie: Original equipment from the factory, but not necessarily original to the vehicle on which the part is currently installed. Slang for "genuine."

gow job: Original term used to describe what we now call a "hot rod." There are several theories regarding where the term originated, the most common of which is that it came from people exclaiming, "Look at that car go!"

grille shell: Protective metal covering for an early automobile's radiator to prevent damage from rocks and other road debris.

header: Streamlined exhaust tubing used to efficiently route spent exhaust gases out of the engine and into the atmosphere. In most cases, they are more efficient than factory exhaust manifolds.

Hemi: Engine in which the combustion chamber is hemispherical (meaning "half circle") in shape, allowing for hotter and more efficient combustion. Although Hemis are produced by several manufacturers around the world, in hot-rodding circles the term refers exclusively to those produced by Chrysler Corporation. The first iteration or "early" Hemi was produced from 1951 to 1958. The second, more powerful, version was produced from 1964 to 1971.

highboy: Fenderless, but not lowered, prewar hot rod.

honey hole: Slang term for any location that yields high-demand and/or high-value automobile cars/parts.

hydros: Slang term for the hydraulic systems that have been integrated into automobile suspensions in order to raise and lower the vehicle. Usually associated with lowriders.

juice brakes: Hydraulic braking system that utilizes hydraulic fluid to activate the brake pads or brake shoes. A common conversion on prewar cars that came equipped with mechanical brakes

kustom: Reference to cars customized from about 1946 until the 1960s. The "k" in "kustom" is said to have been originated by George Barris, one of the early pioneers of car customization.

ladder bars: Suspension component used to prevent wheel hop under hard acceleration in vehicles equipped with coil-spring rear suspensions. Its name comes from its physical resemblance to a ladder.

lakes pipes: Exhaust pipes that are routed along the bottom of the body beneath the doors. They were designed to be easily uncapped to decrease backpressure when racing on dry lakes, thus the term "lakes pipes."

lay frame: To lower a vehicle via airbags or hydraulics until the vehicle's frame rests on the ground.

lead sled: Heavily customized vehicle in which large amounts of lead were used to smooth the customized parts of the body. The extreme weight of the lead was hugely detrimental to the vehicles' performance, comparing their lackadaisical performance to that of a sled.

lowering blocks: Blocks of metal placed between the axle tubes and leaf springs to lower the rear of the vehicle.

lowrider: Full-size American cars that have been altered to ride lower than factory specifications through the use of hydraulics, air bags, lowering blocks, altering coil springs, or other means. Immaculate paint jobs, ornate interiors, the heavy use of chrome, and undersized wheels and tires help to differentiate a lowrider from a vehicle that has merely been lowered.

mechanical brakes: Braking force that is applied mechanically, which is less reliable and less efficient than hydraulically.

Model A: In the hot-rodding world, this refers to Fords produced between the model years 1928 and 1931, not those also known as "Model As" produced between 1903 and 1904. Also called an "A-bone."

Model T: Fords produced between the model years 1908 and 1927.

Mopar: Vehicles produced under the umbrella of Chrysler Corporation. These include Chrysler and Dodge, as well as orphan makes Plymouth and DeSoto. Some also choose to include those made by American Motors Corporation, or AMC, because AMC was absorbed into Chrysler Corporation in the 1980s.

nailhead: V-8 engine produced by Buick from 1953 to 1966. The defining characteristics are its small valves (resembling nails), its vertical valve covers, and its distinctive lopey idle. It is a popular engine for hot rods and rat rods because of its distinct appearance and prodigious output in the larger displacement versions like the 401 and 425.

nose: To remove the chrome from the hood of a vehicle.

OHV: Overhead valve engine, so called because the exhaust and intake valves reside in the heads, not the block.

orphan: Automotive make that is no longer produced, such as DeSoto, LaSalle, Studebaker, and Plymouth.

patina: Natural wear on an object over time. Original patina is among the most desirable traits of a true rat rod.

pentastar: Iconic symbol of cars built by the Chrysler Corporation, sometimes used to denote a vehicle built by Chrysler.

pie crust: Type of racing tire characterized by the distinct scalloping along the outer circumference, reminiscent of the edge of a pie.

piston: Part of the engine that receives the force of the combustion caused by the ignition of the air/fuel mixture. The reciprocating motion of the piston is converted by the crankshaft into rotational motion.

Poncho: Slang term referring to anything Pontiac-related.

Powerglide: Two-speed automatic transmission produced by General Motors. Highly popular among drag racers.

Powerstroke: Line of diesel engines produced by Ford. It's another popular engine conversion seen in rat rods.

psychobilly: Blend of music that combines punk and rockabilly. It's infused with references to science fiction, horror films, and lurid sexuality, among other things.

quick change rear: Rear differential configuration designed for quick gear ratio changes.

rat rod: Quintessential, blue-collar hot rod. Typically a pre-1960 vehicle built on an everyman's budget. Shiny paint is generally verboten, and original wear, tear, and rust are celebrated. Modern additions for the sake of safety and reliability are strongly encouraged, however.

roadster: Open, two-seat car.

rockabilly: One of the earliest forms of rock-and-roll. Often described as a blend of rock and country music.

rolling coal: Tuning the injector pump on a diesel-powered engine so it spews a large, black cloud under full throttle.

RPU: Abbreviation for a roadster pickup.

SBC: Abbreviation for small block Chevy, a smaller displacement engine produced by Chevrolet. Common sizes (in cubic-inch displacement) are 265, 283, 307, 327 and 350. Also known as a "Mouse" motor, regardless of whether or not it is used in a rat rod.

scallops: Kustom painting technique that became popular in the 1950s. Usually done in a matte or "suede" finish on rat rods instead of the shiny finish normally found on kustoms.

scrub line: Imaginary line drawn from the lowest point of the rim diameter of one wheel to the bottom of the tire on the opposite wheel. In theory, in the event of a catastrophic loss of tire pressure, no part of the suspension or drivetrain should touch the ground if the car is built properly.

section: The removal of material from the vertical sheetmetal of a vehicle's body to streamline its appearance.

shave: To remove the chrome trim from the side of a vehicle's body. This can include such things as door handles and locks.

shiner: Shiny, painted, highly detailed hot rod, kustom, or muscle car. Antithesis of a rat rod.

shoebox: Nickname for the streamlined 1949–1951 Fords. Their simple, blocky design was reminiscent of a shoebox, while at the same time they were revolutionary in their design with the use of integrated fenders.

slammed: Used to describe the stance of any vehicle that has been substantially lowered.

slant six: Inline six-cylinder engine produced by the Chrysler Corporation that was designed to rest at a 30-degree angle, which allowed for a lower hoodline. It was produced in huge numbers from 1959–2000. It has earned a phenomenal reputation for reliability and is a great choice for those who want to build a rat rod that stands out from the crowd.

stovebolt: Nickname for the Chevrolet inline six-cylinder engine, so called because the valve cover, lifter cover, and timing cover all utilize a fastener that resembles a stovebolt, which is a slotted-head bolt used in the assembly of some wood-burning stoves.

straight eight: Any inline eight-cylinder engine.

straight pipes: Exhaust system devoid of any mufflers or resonators from the exhaust manifolds to the exhaust tips.

straight six (six-banger): Inline six-cylinder engine.

Stromborgs: Brand of early high-performance carburetors.

suicide doors: Vehicle doors hinged at the rear instead of the front. So called because anybody caught with the door open while the vehicle was moving stood a greater chance of being jettisoned from the vehicle.

suicide front end: Prewar front suspension connected directly to the front of the vehicle frame rather than under it. So called because if the front suspension ever failed, the front of the frame could dig into the road at speed, violently pitching the entire vehicle forward.

suped up (souped up): Refers to a vehicle that has had enhancements made to its performance. Originally spelled as "suped" up (as in super), the spelling has migrated to that of the homophone "souped" up.

three on the tree: Three-speed manual transmission with the gearshift located on the steering column.

toploader: Manual transmission produced by Ford Motor Company in which the gears are replaced and repaired via an access plate on the top of the transmission.

Torqueflite: Three-speed automatic transmission produced by the Chrysler Corporation. Its durability is legendary, and it was credited as being the first automatic transmission that could outperform a manual gearbox at the dragstrip.

tuck 'n' roll: Custom style of upholstery characterized by long vertical pleats.

turbocharger: System of forced induction similar to a supercharger, but instead of being mechanically driven, it is driven by spent exhaust gases.

valve: Part of an engine that directs the flow of the incoming mixture of air and fuel as well as the resulting flow of spent gases out of the combustion chamber.

wedge: Series of big-block engines produced by the Chrysler Corporation, so named for its wedge-shaped combustion chambers. Common sizes (in cubic-inch displacement) are 361, 383, 413, 426, and 440.

Windsor: Series of small-block Ford engines produced at Ford's Windsor, Ontario, plant. Common sizes (in cubic-inch displacement) are 221, 255, 260, 289, 302, and 351.

Z: To modify the frame either in the front or the rear in such a way that, when viewing it in profile, it looks somewhat like the letter "Z." It gives the suspension a higher mounting point, and thus the vehicle sits lower.

zoomie: Single pipes that scavenge spent exhaust gases from an engine. They are different from headers and exhaust manifolds in that each cylinder has its own unique pipe that does not terminate in a common collector or other exit point.

Index

Page numbers in **bold** font indicate an illustration.

Photo Credits

Front Cover: Chad Truss
Back cover: Chad Truss and Sepp Weinzetl

chippix/Shutterstock, 14
Chris Curtis/Shutterstock, 15
Bryan Dagel, 202-207, 201-212, 214-224
Jeff Eatley, 63, 64
FooTToo/Shutterstock, 129
freelanceartist/Shutterstock, 146
Tim Jewett (illustration), 225
johnbraid/Shutterstock, 10
Steve Lagreca/Shutterstock, 16
Tyler Linner (illustration), 200
NguyenLuong Pictures/Shutterstock, 25
Christie Pardini/Shutterstock, 7 (background only)
Tommy Ring, 150-152, 154, 157, 158, 161, 165, 166, 169, 170, 175, 176, 179-181,
    183, 184, 186, 189-193, 195, 196
Jerry Ripley, 2, 62, 74-76, 78- 80 (bottom), 81, 82, 83, 117
Nick Sinclair (illustrations), 19, 58
Richard Thornton, 17
Jeff Thrower/Shutterstock, 92
Chad Truss, 3, 8-9, 20, 22, 23, 26, 29, 31, 32, 34, 38, 40-41, 43-45, 47-49,
    50-53, 55-57, 59-61, 65, 66, 68-71, 73, 84, 86-90, 93-96, 99, 100-104, 107,
    109, 111, 119, 102-122, 124-126, 128, 130, 132-145, 148, 198, 199
Chris Walker, 80 (top)
Walking-onstreet/Shutterstock, 4
Sepp Weinzetl, 115
Dale Wigget, 36-37, 112
Rob Wilson/Shutterstock, 13